THE CHRISTIAN MESSAGE
FOR THE WORLD TODAY

The Group Responsible for This Book

E. STANLEY JONES
KENNETH SCOTT LATOURETTE
JOHN A. MACKAY
FRANCIS J. McCONNELL
BASIL MATHEWS
FRANCIS P. MILLER
WILLIAM PATON
HENRY P. VAN DUSEN
LUTHER ALLAN WEIGLE
A. L. WARNSHUIS, *Chairman*

THE CHRISTIAN MESSAGE
FOR THE WORLD TODAY

*A Joint Statement of the
World-Wide Mission of
the Christian Church*

Essay Index Reprint Series

 BOOKS FOR LIBRARIES PRESS
FREEPORT, NEW YORK

First Published 1934
Reprinted 1971

INTERNATIONAL STANDARD BOOK NUMBER:
0-8369-2184-4

LIBRARY OF CONGRESS CATALOG CARD NUMBER:
77-152163

PRINTED IN THE UNITED STATES OF AMERICA

FOREWORD

T HIS is a book which no one person could write. The forces with which it deals are too complex and the message it attempts to state is too great to be trusted to individual expression.

Naturally those of us who have collaborated in the writing of the book hold divergent views on some of the matters considered. At certain basic points, however, we have found ourselves standing together on common ground.

We are agreed in our view of the gravity of the present world situation. We look upon a world shaken to its foundations, a world in which forces of greed and hate and divisiveness have run amuck. We are deeply concerned lest these forces remain out of control and hurl society back into an age of darkness from which it will take centuries to emerge.

We are agreed in finding Jesus Christ to be the key to the meaning of life and of the universe. We discover in Him the truth about the nature of ultimate reality. We regard Him not merely as a great teacher but as the self-revelation of the very heart of God. Any lesser gospel we regard as inadequate to sustain a Christian world movement.

We are agreed in our conviction about the unique and universal significance of Jesus Christ. What He means to us we hold He may mean to all men everywhere. Gratefully recognizing the important values to be found in other re-

7

ligions, and eagerly desiring to cooperate with all men of spiritual insight, we are persuaded that in conscious fellowship with God as revealed in Christ and commitment to His purposes lies the pathway to the highest life.

We are agreed in regarding evangelism—the witness to what Christ means to us—as the heart of our missionary task. We believe in an evangelism of both word and deed. While we regard the testimony of life as the decisive thing, without which any words will be weak and futile, we are convinced that a true understanding and acceptance of the significance of Jesus Christ for the world is the foundation of all the beneficent influences that flow from the missionary movement.

We are agreed in holding that Christian missions looks toward the creation of a world society permeated in every aspect of its life by the spirit of Jesus Christ. That society is to be one in which love prevails, breaking down divisive barriers between nation and nation, race and race, class and class. We hold no easy-going optimism about human progress; we are painfully aware that we can maintain this vision of the outcome only by a heroic venture of faith. But the Christian church, by reason of its very gospel, can do no less than witness to and work for such a society.

We are agreed that if there is to be such a world fellowship it must be built upon Jesus Christ as the cornerstone. If spiritual forces are to prevail over the forces of selfish materialism, it will be because the world finds in Jesus Christ the supreme redeeming force in history.

We are agreed in our conviction as to the central importance of the church. While heirs to different historic forms of church organization, we are one in regarding the Church as truly the "Body of Christ," the great fellowship binding together across the ages all those who have found in Christ the true meaning of life, and carrying forward His spirit and purpose from generation to generation.

There is a timelessness in the Christian gospel but the timeless gospel has to be proclaimed to an age that has its own dominating forms of thought and life. We therefore examine, first, some of the most crucial aspects of the world as we see it today—a world of men whose high hopes have been chilled into disillusionment, a world in which powerful new forces like nationalism and Communism are claiming the allegiance of millions, a world in which the economic order is shaken as by an earthquake, a world in which age-old social structures are breaking up.

Facing such a world with the common convictions we hold and drawn together by a common devotion to the world mission of Christianity in this age of universal change and transformation, we have endeavored to set forth a message rooted in the imperishable truth of Christ and relevant to the problems of today and tomorrow.

(*Signed*) E. STANLEY JONES
KENNETH SCOTT LATOURETTE
JOHN A. MACKAY
FRANCIS J. McCONNELL
BASIL MATHEWS
FRANCIS P. MILLER
WILLIAM PATON
HENRY P. VAN DUSEN
LUTHER ALLAN WEIGLE
A. L. WARNSHUIS, *Chairman*

CONTENTS

I.

THE WORLD TODAY

The Chapters of this section were prepared by

I. Henry P. Van Dusen
II. Basil Mathews
III. Francis P. Miller
IV. Francis J. McConnell

I.

THE MOOD OF OUR GENERATION

THE man of today is a child of the modern age. He has been born into a world preformed for his advent. He has been suckled and reared within its life—a home comfortably appointed for his nurture, lavishly responsive to his desires, proudly conscious of his importance, confidently expectant of his future. As youth has matured and he has taken on manhood, he has tasted of its pleasures; he has discovered its convictions; he has been initiated into its assumptions, its ambitions, its hopes. He has found them good. And so they have become organically ingrafted within his own life, part and parcel of his inmost being. Today he is a faithful reflection of the times which have given him birth.

To his natural parents he has not always responded so uncritically. Maturing experiences have brought comparison with other and better parents, illumination from modern psychology, the devastating contrast between his own upbringing and that which he intends for his children. He has been unable to stifle a resentful revolt against his inadequate rearing. The outcome is the familiar hiatus between the older and younger generations. But from his social parentage he has experienced no such alienation. For one thing, the instruments of criticism are not his. There is no alternative parentage which might suggest unfavorable comparison. He knows nothing of history; therefore he has no calculus for judgment between his own heritage and those of earlier generations. Further, he finds his world comfortable, exciting, eminently satisfactory; there is no inner stimulus to criticism. If, in recent months, a shadow of distrust has crept across his attitude toward his world, it is a very late appearance. For the most part, the man of today is not only a faithful reflection of the modern age but also its grateful and ardent eulogist.

II.

In the advance of that modern age, three parallel phases may be clearly distinguished. To be sure, they developed simultaneously, acting and reacting upon one another continuously. They appear as three aspects of a single movement, but to distinguish them aids a clear understanding of the modern scene. We may speak of them as *Modern Life, Modern Thought,* and the *Modern Mood.*

In *Modern Life* we see the objective setting of the age, the more obvious and external circumstances of men's life —the development of invention, of technology and of transportation as they have modified these circumstances; the events which attracted men's interest and registered their history; the concerns which claimed their devotion and furnished their satisfactions.

By *Modern Thought* we mean the consciously developed philosophies of the period—developed and prized largely by the infinitesimal company of the "intelligentsia," and never as influential as the few suppose. For it has not been the articulate philosophies of the schools but factors far more subtile and submerged which, all through the modern period, have been determining the inner mood of the common man —the half-understood feelings and half-articulated convictions and half-recognized presuppositions which are *his* philosophy of life—all we mean by the familiar phrase, the *Modern Mood.*

It is this last, the *Modern Mood,* which is the major object of our interest. But a rapid survey of its companion factors will prepare the way for a clearer grasp of its development and its present currents.

III.

To interpret the life of any period, most of all the complex and confused panorama of the modern scene, in terms of a single influence, must always smack of over-simplification. But few would question that there is one preeminently significant key to the development of the world's life in the past century—*the advance of man's effective mastery over Nature.*

The tale is too familiar, too threadbare to permit retelling again. We sicken of the reiterated statistics, the inapprehensible comparisons, and our fatigued imaginations refuse to stir to a fresh grasping of it all. The facts remain, none the less. They have been given graphic and definitive portraiture in the Century of Progress exposition. The most flagging imagination and blasé attention must be stabbed awake by its story. Whether one hail it as a consummate representation of mankind's preeminent achievement or view it as a depressing symbol of our preoccupation with the cheap and the material, the truth of history which it tells is unmistakable.

17

Each man's life in any age is compact of two great sets of factors. The one, the external circumstances of his life and the events which befall him, differ from age to age and mark each man's date, each generation's distinctive history. The other, the primordial forces within his own soul and the problems they beget, he largely shares with all mankind; they vary little from age to age. Of the two great factors which determine men's life, one—the first—has suffered more radical transformation within the life-time of our generation than in all of human history before.

The external setting of the life of every inhabitant of the western world today—all that surrounds his spirit and makes incessant impact upon it, molding and fashioning it beyond his realization—is more completely different from that of his grandfather than was his grandfather's from that of Socrates. It is a new creation. That fact is sufficient to determine the key to *Modern Life*.

The by-products of all this are likewise a tale too familiar. Let us speak of four:

a. The advance of man's effective mastery over Nature has accomplished the unification of the world. Through multiplied and instant communication, through the dispersion of information and education and culture, through interlocking commercial and financial equity, the peoples of the world live in continuous and intimate contact with one another; and their common interest is largely one. *And* this unification has found its most significant expression in— the World War.

b. The advance of man's effective mastery over Nature has, for the first time in human history, made thoroughly practicable adequate food, shelter, security, education, recreation and a modest comfort for every citizen of the Western world. *And* that possibility has taken actuality in—the present depression.

c. The advance of man's effective mastery over Nature has opened wide the doorway to culture, acquaintance with the rich treasures of man's past, participation in the delicate and deep imponderables of the human spirit, for all who will enter. *And* the most general response to that invitation has been—the movies, the radio, jazz.

d. Most significant, the advance of man's effective mastery over Nature has promised the modern man achievements and satisfactions beyond the dreams of his forebears. *And* that promise has found realization in—the typical, "successful" American of today—superficial, crude, blatant, inwardly uncertain and unhappy.

The promise—a united world, security and comfort, culture, happiness. The fulfillment—a World War, the depression, jazz, ennui. A partial and one-sided picture, to be sure; one thread among many. But will anyone question that it is the dominant character of the portrait, the central thread in the tangled skein which is *Modern Life?*

IV.

Modern Thought is a term loosely employed. It may bear one of two meanings. Frequently men intend to indicate by it the general temper of the times—the presuppositions and convictions and ideals of the man in the street, which we prefer to designate as the *Modern Mood*. More strictly *Modern Thought* should refer to the consciously and deliberately formulated philosophies of the age.

Here also, amid the eddies and currents of intellectual controversy in the past century, it is not difficult to fasten upon the single major key to the development. One problem, thrusting itself into prominence early in the century and gaining centrality in men's thinking increasingly as the modern movement advanced, has furnished the setting, determined the issues, and in large measure dictated the terms of philosophic discussion. It is *the relation of science to traditional tenets*.

The great preoccupation of thought has been to agree upon the meaning of modern science for philosophy. The main issues of debate have sprung from seeming conflicts between the implications of science and generally accepted assumptions. The newer schools, consolidating an ever firmer preeminence, have made their aim the complete and final displacement of older views by a "scientific philosophy." In passing let it be noted that by a "scientific philosophy" either of two objectives may be indicated—the erection of a quite new philosophy from *materials* supplied solely by the particular sciences, discarding such traditional materials as technical science is not prepared to handle; or the reconstruction of philosophy from both old and new materials by employment of a new *method* derived from science. But whether science was recognized as furnishing both materials and methods for sound philosophy, or method only, it was science which was dictating the terms of the modern intellectual quest.

The results of this ascendency of a scientific outlook and methodology are not difficult to define. Inevitably, it focused the attention of thought upon those aspects of reality and of human experience with which science could most readily deal, to the neglect or denial of other aspects which eluded scientific categories. That meant a concentration upon the general rather than the individual, the primitive rather than the mature, the uniform rather than the unique, the familiar rather than the original, the commonplace rather than the delicate, the rare, the meaningful, the profound. In brief, it fostered and glorified a perspective directly antipodal to that which the nobler philosophies had made their own; and a preoccupation with data at precisely the opposite pole from that which these philosophies had learned to recognize as most significant.[1]

So much is obvious. Few would question it. But it is too simple and therefore too superficial a rendering of the matter. It was not only the intellectual principles and conclusions of science which were vitally effective in determining the development of *Modern Thought*. Even more influential was the character of world-life which science was making possible and with the actual erection of which it was tirelessly preoccupied.

Ideally it is philosophy's distinctive function to criticize the culture of the day in the light of higher and truer perspectives. In reality it rises to that high vocation but rarely, at moments of great intellectual and spiritual creativity. More frequently, it takes its cue from prevailing popular enthusiasms instead of from the wealth of its own historic treasures.

---

[1] See Henry P. Van Dusen, *The Plain Man Seeks for God*, pp. 55-64. See also, Joseph Needham, *The Great Amphibium*, Ch. I.

And the outcome of its labors is not the correction of prevailing assumptions by the touchstone of wider truths, but a rationalization of those assumptions into intellectual respectibility. Thought becomes the servile handmaiden of that to which it should be relentless tutor. This is the story of philosophy in the past century.[2]

It is a not untrue characterization of the regnant schools to suggest that their subconscious, and probably controlling, motivation was to develop a view of things which should be thoroughly harmonious with the dominant temper of *Modern Life*. Not so much consistency with scientific theory as congruity with contemporary life was the great concern. Like the man in the street, the philosopher found his world good; he yearned to outfit it with respectable and impressive intellectual dress. And so a discerning eye detects philosophy throughout the period scuffling in confused and undignified haste to effect a tardy adjustment to the interests, desires and presuppositions of the life of the day.

Modern Life was intensely absorbed in the techniques and externals and appurtenances of living, relatively oblivious of its delicate and personal inner apprehensions; so *Thought* became. *Modern Life* found its great ally and servant in technical science and, like the lion in John Masefield's *Son of Adam,* was soon imprisoned within science's skilfully wrought mechanisms; *Thought* followed suit and suffered like imprisonment. *Modern Life* fastened men's admiring attention upon their own abilities and accomplishments, fostering in them a quite exaggerated self-importance and

---

[2] This point has been developed with compelling cogency by Professar Whitehead in his *Science and the Modern World,* espec. Chs. V and VI.

illusory self-security; *Modern Thought* translated this habitual attitude into a self-conscious theory of reality.

In brief, the philosophies most characteristic of the time became increasingly pallid and rather pitiable reflections of the actual character of the society in which they dwelt—naturalistic, materialistic, humanistic, pragmatistic, and above all supine and sterile. In wide circles thought gave over its responsibility of criticism and correction for the easier if somewhat ludicrous role of accommodation and imitation.[3]

V.

From the point of view of our special interest—religion's status in the life of today—two parenthetical comments must be interjected.

Our analysis has concerned secular life and thought. It should be unnecessary to add that, at almost every point, religion has shared fully the dominant features of the Modern Age. To a sensitive and candid churchman, the description of the life and thought of these times is self-portraiture.[4]

The life of the church has drunk deep of the enthusiasms

[3] On the parallel development and mutual influence of theory and practical life during the modern period, see especially Paul Tillich, *The Religious Situation* (tr. H. R. Niebuhr)—an indispensable source for anyone who would understand the life of today. There the spiritually powerful influences are listed as three: mathematical natural science, technology, the prevailing economy. These three; and the greatest of these is the last.

[4] As Tillich well points out, the factors which have been determining spiritual developments during the modern period can most readily be detected in the great areas of secular concern—in art, literature, science, politics and common life—and they may there be most significantly revealed. That is another way of indicating the servility of formal religion to the temper of the times.

of the secular world and fallen heavily under the spell of its assumptions and its ideals. Bigger and grander churches, more and cleverer mechanical contrivances, larger and more inflated budgets, sermon-topics inspired by newspaper headlines, sermon-treatment guided by advertising technique, sermon-results tested by external and numerical computation, the aims of the church defined in harmony with prevailing secular goals, the power of the church measured by accepted business norms—the modern church has been fully within the fabric of *Modern Life* and has been jubilantly faithful to its central temper.

And the thought of the churches, their theology? We have pictured *Modern Thought* in undignified scuttle to "keep up with the Joneses" of *Modern Life*. How could one draw a true portrait of the most advanced Christian thinking except in that posture so familiar to us all—scurrying in precipitate and breathless embarrassment to bring the interpretation of religion into conformity with the latest conclusions of secular thought? We have urged that it is the special task of philosophy to guide, not to follow, current trends, to correct, not obey, their assumptions. How much more is it the bounden duty of religion to stand apart from the transient aberrations and presumptions of the moment and bring them under the judgment of its own higher insights. To fail in that responsibility is to stand without excuse. And it is to ring religion's own death-knell.

VI.

Again, from the point of view of religion's status in the thought of today, the more recent tendencies must not be taken too seriously. A longer perspective is demanded. In that perspective, it is clear that scientific thought and scientific civilization have not created the problem; they have accentuated it and given it the particular form in which contemporary man sees it. With all of the revolutionary developments of the Nineteenth Century, the situation of Christianity—both its intellectual defense and its popular effectiveness—was not greatly different at the close of the century from what it had been at the beginning of that century. Indeed, the parallel between the two century-turns is arresting.

It has been pointed out that the Eighteenth Century left religion "apparently helpless in the face of the rationalistic attack." To recall the plight of the church at that period is almost to imagine one is viewing the situation of the church today. It was a temporary discomfiture, however. So extreme a rationalism and scepticism as that which dominated thought at the close of the Eighteenth Century bred an inevitable reaction. Through the united impact of the Wesleyan revival, the Romantic movement, and the rehabilitation of intuition and faith, religion experienced a recovery of confidence in message and power in society. Our grandfathers dwelt in an "age of faith." Only later came the impact of modern science as we know it. And the history of the preceding century was repeated in almost identical terms.

The point is that the tension in which Christian thought finds itself in our time is not solely a feature of the scientific age. It has been characteristic of the past three centuries rather than of the last century alone. It springs from conflict between the Christian view of man and the world and another view which long antedated modern science but which has hailed the "scientific viewpoint" as a ready ally.

And the issues of that tension, while they present themselves to the man of today in the dress determined by scientific thought, are essentially the same—a philosophy seeking to encompass all of reality with its fathomless depth and richness and variety or a philosophy based upon selective abstraction; the search for truth with every faculty of the human spirit, or with the processes of logical inductive reason alone; the assertion of man's centrality in creation and unbounded confidence in man's powers both to know and to do, or the recognition of man's finiteness before the majesty and mystery of the universe in which his lot is cast and a humble confession of man's limited powers to know and his tragically faltering willingness to do the right.

VII.

In such a setting of world-life and thought-world we discover the man of today. They have bred and nurtured him. What shall we say of him, and of his convictions, his assumptions, his hopes, his misgivings—all that constitutes the *Modern Mood?*

The main meaning of what has gone before is clear enough. Like the plain man of any age, the convictions of the man of today have been taken up bodily out of the life of the times into which he happens to have been born. His most secure premises are, in overwhelming majority, uncriticized reflections of the prevailing interests and hopes of his society. Three major influences the modern age has had upon his attitudes and his feeling for life. It has severed his living connection with the past; it has fastened his hopes in the machine; it has fostered a consciousness of unprecedented human autonomy and power.

Not only has the temper of the age encouraged a disdain of tradition and the riches of history; for the average man it has actually severed a vital connection with that past. A few years ago a well-known professor of psychology was fond of telling his students that he could not understand why anyone should recommend a text-book in any subject written more than fifteen years previously—the year in which he first began to teach behavioristic psychology. That is an absurd exaggeration of the dominant attitude of the *Modern Mood*.

Poor deluded man! If only he could be persuaded to turn the pages of the history he so despises, he would see his prototype in 400 B.C., again in the age of Augustus, in 350 A.D., at the Renaissance, in the middle of the Eighteenth Century—each man equally supercilious toward the past, equally certain that knowledge would henceforth be dated from his age. And he would see, also, the long sweeping tides of history carry his prototypes away and make of them and their ages but flickering specks in the ebb and flow of man's age-long search for truth.

As we have said, the man of today knows no history; he has been led to think history unimportant. He knows nothing of the underlying corporate psychological forces which so largely determine any age and those who live in it. He has no understanding of the great cyclic movements of action and reaction in man's thought and man's progress which determine that periods of great idealism are succeeded by times of blunt realism; that romanticism and emotionalism and optimism make way for conservatism, dogmatism, reaction; that sophistication is usually followed by moral sterility; that high prosperity gives birth to superficiality, then arrogance, then disillusionment, then disgust with the world, then cynicism, then moral decline, and finally disintegration and retrogression.

He lacks the first mark of education and the prerequisite to culture—historic perspective. Therefore he has no equipment, if he desired it, to locate the significance of his own day in the drama of history and, thereby, to judge and correct his own instinctive assumptions. In brief, he has no understanding of the day in which he lives. By the same token, he possesses no valid vision for the future, no grasp of the course ahead which progress must take, if there is to be progress. And no commanding passion that the stuff of this present shall be molded into the possibilities of that visioned future.

In similar fashion, he is spiritually impoverished, divorced from the sources of a significant culture. We have thought to build a culture out of modern life. But, even if the materials for the enhancement of culture were present (and that is by no means certain), one cannot build a culture over night, one cannot build a culture *de novo,* one cannot build a culture out of machinery and household conveniences, one cannot *build* a culture at all. It must grow. And it must grow from soil rich and fallow for its nurture, by the slow processes of natural development and enrichment. In American life there were seedplots from which a sound and significant culture might have flowered. The early American tradition, especially in New England, was fertile in rootage for a national culture. Indeed it had given unmistakable promise for the future in the preliminary flowering of the Golden Day of American literature and art. And there were other hopeful seedplots in the frontier tradition and elsewhere. But the whole impact of modern life has tended to cut connection with that tradition, to breed disdain of it and its possible gifts for life, to relegate all pre-machine-age achievements to the museum of antiquities, and to advertise

28

the "new culture" which science and the machine and modern man together would construct.

And so the man in the street stands today rootless—a prodigious, overgrown, adolescent sapling—swayed by every wind of doctrine, without the rootage which might have furnished him with security and stability against the blizzards and devastating simoons of the times and without the deep satisfactions which are possible to firmly founded men in any age.

Again, the modern age has fastened his hopes in the machine. As I have elsewhere suggested, "It has fixed his attention upon the amassing of things, the multiplication of accoutrements, the perfecting of appliances and contrivances. It has persuaded him that plumbing is more important than poetry, facts than understanding, the latest than the best, standardization than individuality, quantity output than originality, success than life." It was significant that, with all the furore of alarm over Technocracy, almost no one raised question at its fundamental premise—that, since machinery can steadily increase output with diminishing human labor, there will be less and less work for men to do.

But machinery cannot paint Sistine Madonnas; machinery cannot produce handcraft; machinery cannot erect Chartres cathedrals, as many of our contemporary churches abundantly testify. It is obvious that machinery is powerless to supply to the life of man any gift where worth attaches to richness and depth, to originality and subtlety and individuality. And it is powerless to furnish channels through which all that is most delicate and personal and profound in human aspiration and insight might find expression. It is some measure of the spiritual reality and fertility of the *Modern*

29

Mood that it contemplated with confident satisfaction a machine-made civilization.

Finally, the modern age has fostered in its children a consciousness of unprecedented human autonomy and almost unlimited power. This was the inevitable result of its influence at every point. By creating a new world of outward circumstance, it suggested that a new order of men had appeared as authors and sovereigns of that world. By providing tools of size and speed and power it imputed vicarious greatness and strength to those who wield them. By enclosing men within the satisfactions of their machine-dominated life and away from nature's immensities and mysteries, it foreshortened perspective and fostered a grotesque self-importance. By severing contact with the riches of earlier human achievement, it prevented comparisons which might have induced more intelligent humility. By magnifying genuine accomplishments in a single aspect of experience it encouraged the impression of mastery over every problem. By fastening an intent attention upon step-by-step advance in the chosen path, it created the illusion of general progress and blinded men to the precipices inevitably ahead.

Nothing seemed able so much as to joggle man's unbridled self-confidence—not the war, the most gigantic corporate folly in all human history; nor even the depression, inevitable fruit of the most blatant stupidity and greed in civilized times. Modern man "burns incense to himself and his own countenance is hidden from him in the smoke."

These are the outward features of the *Modern Mood*. Nevertheless, to describe them only is to give a quite false impression of the deeper and hidden temper of that *Mood*. We have already suggested that one of the most characteristic expressions of the age was jazz. Would anyone who has moved freely in the midstream of the world's life through these recent years question it? But what is jazz? Jazz which Walter Horton has so acutely analyzed:

"Jazz is the perfect symbol of our mood: raucous ribaldry on the surface, with a deep undercurrent of the blues, syncopated to conceal the heartbreak, blaring loud dissonant defiance at all who would presume to question the genuineness of its hilarity." [5]

And the bearer of that mood, the typical man of today—"that strange, absurd, pathetic, notable, conquering Hamlet of the modern world, with his catchwords and his motor-cars, a score of platitudes on his lips and a score of unrealized desires in his heart." [6]

Beneath the thin veneer of satisfied self-assurance, the man of today is a strangely bewildered, frustrated, profoundly unhappy mortal.

VIII.

But that is not the final word.

If our description truly portrays the life and mood of today, or even of yesterday, it is a day which to tomorrow's view will seem a dead and distant past. The *Modern Mood* with all its baggage of presuppositions and pretensions is disappearing under our eyes. It is disappearing under a twofold influence—disintegration within and devastating attack from without.

---

[5] Walter M. Horton, *Theism and the Modern Mood*, p. 7.
[6] Struthers Burt.

A few years ago, visitors from abroad reported that in Europe men were becoming uncertain in their own autonomy. Then, that uncertainty found no echo in American life. To-day, we confront a generation shorn of self-confidence—disillusioned of its own leadership, disillusioned as to the significance of its own achievement, disillusioned of its power to save the crumbling remnants of its proud domain. The florid optimism of yesterday has evaporated overnight. A new situation has lowered upon us like a dark and sudden squall on spanking, sparkling wavelets. It demands new equipment and new skills. As a ship caught unprepared heaves to clumsily to reef in the teeth of the storm, men are searching their souls to test their adequacy for the demands of a new day.

A craving for authority is gnawing more and more at men's spirits. Our generation knows it has been betrayed. And, if the betrayal is of its own making, the bitterness is no less on that account. The leadership, the assumptions, the dominant institutions of the modern age stand under severe condemnation. And, in so far as they partook of the follies of that age, the church and the cause of religion share in that condemnation. Sir Michael Sadler, describing prevailing attitudes among Oxford undergraduates, says: "The young are eager and hungry—for faith, for work, for a leader whom they can trust and follow without question. . . . They are not interested in what at one time I would have gone to the stake for—I mean liberty of thought. Give them the possibility of ardor in achievement and they would not care a hang about—for example—the freedom of the press. . . . Once the young have found their leader and accepted his purpose, there will be a revolution." There, one suspects, is the mood of tomorrow.

But to the facts of internal disintegration must be added the factors of external attack. Across the world today there are forces powerfully at play which are dissolving the *Modern Mood* like cheap amalgam under strong acid. And the acids which are purging and testing the world's life are far more potent, far more irresistible than the famed "acids of modernity." There are causes and faiths powerfully clamant for men's allegiance. But they bear not the slightest resemblance to the attitudes and movements which have been alluring the man of today throughout the modern period.

In every corner of the world, two such faiths are foremost —nationalism and Communism. They do not invite participation; they command allegiance. They do not persuade to hypotheses; they declare finalities. They do not encourage discussion; they silence criticism. They do not promise satisfactions; they demand sacrifice. They do not pamper men; they conscript their very souls. They do not magnify the individual; they require his all in the service of the whole. But from that complete self-giving they propose to build a new world for all mankind.

These are the forces which press their commands upon the man of today. His mind, lulled by the comforting self-inflation and easy-going agnosticisms of the modern age, is ill-tempered for the challenge of their confident dogmatisms. His life, made flabby in the lush worldliness of modern life, is ill-prepared for the rigors of their discipline. In the face of these dogmatic and demanding causes, weak men stand vacillating in impotent indecision. Strong men—or those who wish to convey the impression of strength—rush to speedy and unthinking enlistment.

The sum of it all is, the incense of self-glorification which modern men have been burning at their own altar is speedily evaporating. We begin to see ourselves truly at last. And the mirror returns to us a disquietingly stupid and weak and bewildered countenance. Ours is the paralysis of humiliating self-discovery.

The relevance of all that we have been saying for the concern of this volume should be patent. It is to the man of today—a child of the modern age, bitterly disillusioned of his parentage, tragically ill-equipped for the issues of the new day, baffled and nerveless before the onset of the currents of the times—it is to him that the Christian faith must bring its message.

II.

THE GROWING FAITH OF COMMUNISM

A T THE celebration of Peace Day in Moscow, thousands of boys and girls of the Komsomol (the Communist Youth Movement) are massed in the Park of Culture and Rest. They are addressed through loud speakers by Chinese, Japanese, American and other Communists from all over the world, declaring the missionary triumphs of the Bolshevik Revolution. Bugles sound. At this signal they chant in unison, "We are changing the world." Again and again the bugles sound, and Russian youth, thrilled with the conviction of the eventual triumph of their cause around the earth, declare, "We *are* changing the world." After this they file past the embalmed body of Lenin, who lived and died to build that new world. They are taken through the museum.

It strangely recalls the missionary exhibitions of the Christian West. Here are maps of the world in which, as in the missionary maps of thirty years ago, they see the areas converted to the new religion and the "regions beyond," awaiting the missionaries of Communism with indications in China and Japan, India, Persia and Egypt of the successes of the propaganda. The slogan that used to thrill the conventions of the Student Volunteer Movement in America and Britain, "The Evangelization of the World in This Generation," now relegated to a pigeonhole by Western

Christianity, is the declaration of decisive strategy by the new faith of Communism.

These boys and girls of the new Russia have much to inspire them as they hear the actual facts. There is hardly an educational institution in Japan without its secret "cell" of enthusiastic and intellectually equipped Communist students ready for the Revolution. The Japanese government which used to regard the Christian social reformer, Toyohiko Kagawa, askance as a revolutionary and send police to listen in to his addresses, now embarrasses him by encouraging students to hear him. This is not because he has changed, for he has not, but because the "dangerous thoughts movement" in Japan, with Communism as its revolutionary program, makes Kagawa's passion for constitutional social reform acceptable in comparison.

On the map of China these Russian boys and girls are shown areas in which Chinese numbering over fifty million souls are under Red rule. From the plantation workers of the Dutch East Indies in Java to the laborers of the Argentine and the students of Peru, from the civil servants of Mexico to the proletariat of the new industrial revolution in Rhodesia and Bengal, stories converge on Moscow of the missionary successes of Communism.

When we turn back to Communism as a doctrine and to Bolshevism as its first great experiment toward the transition to a complete world-wide socialist society, what do we discover as to the authentic roots of this militant faith? Is it too much to claim that, conceived in terms of this material world, Communism has all the necessary characteristics and commands all the loyalties of a religion? Is it not true that looking across the nations of the world the real competitors with Christianity for the control of the lives of youth are not the old pessimistic faiths of Hinduism and Buddhism, nor the *démodé* rigid citadel of Islam, nor the gentle yet stern scheme of loyalties in Confucianism, but integral nationalism rising to mystical heights in Fascism and the scheme of universal salvation proclaimed by Communism?

Communism has the essential characteristic of a religion in that it proclaims a doctrine and a way of salvation. It is salvation here and now with "beyondness" eliminated. It is salvation universal both in geographical extent for all men and in its inclusive control of all aspects of a man's life. Is this not the first time in history that we see a secular idea issuing in a concrete program of salvation with a total view of the life of man, and claiming universal validity?

This universality is of the essence of the salvation offered or rather promised by Communism. Communism in theory and Bolshevism in practice claim that they must ultimately rule everywhere or nowhere. Bolshevism cannot persist indefinitely in an even partially capitalistic world. Stalin compromised this principle of the pure Marxian and Leninian universal gospel, when he at last succeeded in carrying the project of the Five Year Plan on the plea of making a successful national experiment in Russia first. But the plan was that this was purely an interim nationalism to provide a more efficient home base for a world missionary conquest.

An apocalyptic vision of this saved world is one of the most powerful elements in the faith of Communism. As the author of the Book of Revelation saw the Holy City, the new Jerusalem, coming down from heaven, the City in which sorrow and death would be no more, so young Communists see a planned, cooperative, classless world society of workers. Nor is this simply an apocalypse floating in the cloudy idealism of "wishful" thinking. It is backed by a

37

definite philosophy that gives to Communism the marvelous driving force of a sense of destiny. Karl Marx's doctrine of economic determinism looks cold and remorseless when stated in terms of the irresistible drive of impersonal forces. It arose, as we know, out of Hegel's philosophy of history, his belief in the eternal *process,* the inevitability of progress. But when it is harnessed to a war against economic injustice this determinism takes on that strange fervor which the doctrine of predestination gave to Cromwell's Ironsides.

It is one of the most astonishing paradoxes of actual history that the naive romanticism of Rousseau, caught up philosophically by Kant and developed by Hegel into an almost mystical theory of the state as the appointed channel of this historic process, should have created both a glorification of the nation-state, with war as its tool, and autocracy and subjection as its methods and, when turned upside down by Karl Marx with his doctrine of the Materialistic Conception of History, have inspired the faith of Communism with its sense of destiny. For Hegel the heart of progress was the causal "idea" which was reflected in material things and conditions. Marx inverted this. He saw the material things and conditions and particularly the mechanical equipment or "tools" of man as the cause of progress, because the machine demands new processes of production and therefore new social and economic organization.

These "powers of production," as Karl Marx calls them, compel the industrial capitalists to herd workers into factories and discipline them for production. They thus give the workers the capacity and the chance to organize themselves as a subject class against their masters. Thus the Capitalist class and Capitalism as a system will be the agent of its own destruction and the victorious proletariat will take hold of the tools of production and eliminate the other classes. There will then be no class to be exploited.

The interim dictatorship of the proletariat (essential during the period of world revolution) will give place to a classless society in which all the resources of the community will be controlled in the interests of everyone. This apocalyptic picture of a glorious future makes this theory of economic determinism glow with warmth and light. The forces of the universe are with Communism. The world revolution must swing forward on that tide which no capitalistic King Canute can hold back by an inch. As in Christianity or Islam the believer is obedient to the will of God, so is the Communist consciously submissive to the predetermined process that will bring in the final world-order.

By an odd but often repeated paradox this determinism does not create quietism, but a fierce fighting quality. Oliver Cromwell's Ironsides swinging into battle chanting "Let the Lord arise and His enemies be scattered" were predestinarian Calvinists. They were certain that in the mind of God everything was fixed and preordained, but that did not prevent them from giving their lives with passionate enthusiasm to helping to achieve His ends. Mohammedanism again even rivals Calvinism in the doctrine that what God wills happens, and that what He does not will cannot be brought about. But there never was a faith that drew out such fierce and enthusiastically joyful fighting as the Mohammedan missionary campaigns.

It is similar with this new godless Calvinism of Marx. You can neither hasten nor slacken the pace of the wheels of economic determinism, but the sense of destiny, of irresistible drive is one of the Communists' greatest assets in demanding loyal cooperation even unto death. Communism then is also a religion of faith and hope. Its devotees really believe in these material forces. They are ready to launch into the deep. On joining the Communist Party they declare their readiness to give life or to take life if the "Party" commands it.

This faith of Communism issues in another powerful religious quality, that of belief in the power to change human nature. This change of course is not effected mystically from within. It comes by a change of economic environment. Man is controlled by the profit motive. The reason for this they say is that he has three fears: first, that he may get out of work and therefore he must provide against that contingency; second, that his descendants may suffer and for that reason he amasses profits; and third, that he may fall ill, and be unable to suport himself. All of these three fears would be eliminated in the ideal Communist state. Therefore the acquisitive motive, which is their fruit, goes with them and, in that sense, human nature is to be changed.

Another outstanding religious quality of Communism is its sense of social justice. This was born in Communism at the very outset, for it breathed in Karl Marx. The son of a Jew converted to Christianity, Karl Marx, as Middleton Murry truly says, "is of the company of the Hebrew Prophets." Hegel controlled his head, but Hosea inspired his heart. In Marx the intellectual and the prophetic, the economist and the evangelist found strange unity. What he coldly conceived as "idea" surrounded by books in the Library of the British Museum, he passionately desired in his heart as the son of a Christian-Jew who found first in Isaiah and then in the Sermon on the Mount the highest truth about life. As H. G. Wood says in his *Christianity and Communism,* Marx's hatred of oppression "has its roots, consciously or unconsciously, in Jewish prophecy and the teaching and example of Jesus." [1]

The religiousness of the human and especially the Russian heart has worked a strange revenge upon Lenin's passionate advocacy of a godless creed in making him, in some sort, the Messiah of the new world-order. That little man, who dedicated his life from adolescence with such puritanic intensity to the achievement of the Communist Revolution in his native country, has become, when dead, the Messianic leader whose spirit is more potent today than even when he lived. The mausoleum in the Red Square at Moscow is, as we know, the scene of an incessant pilgrimage of devotees, who pass continuously by his embalmed body.

What is more significant, those who enter freely into the tiny homes of Russian peasants say that you will frequently discover in the little cabin the icon of the old Greek Orthodox Church still hanging on the woman's side of the hut, but on the man's side the picture of Lenin standing triumphantly on the world and with the rising sun radiating its rays behind him like a great halo, the Twentieth Century icon, the godless Messiah. A parallel suggests itself here with Buddhism. Gautama Buddha having contemplated the sorrows of man and the nature of the world-order was unable to discover God, and said so. In revenge the religious intuition of mankind has made the image of the Buddha himself an object of worship across all Asia.

By a similar paradox the Lenin who said "we do not want anything to be accepted with the eyes shut, to be an article of faith. Everyone should keep his head tight on his own shoulders, and think out and verify everything for himself"

[1] Round Table Press, 1933.

has himself become, with Marx the author of infallible scriptures. As Nicholas Berdyaev shows in his article on "The 'General Line' of Soviet Philosophy" [2] there is a continuous and increasing stern heresy hunt in process which excommunicates every deviation of thought from the orthodox line of Marx, Engels, Lenin, and of Stalin. Thus Marx's *Capital* is becoming like Mohammed's Qu'ran, the infallible scripture of a new orthodoxy.

Berdyaev, who has made a close study of the contemporary discussions and was himself a convinced Marxian until his conversion to Christianity, says, "The argument in these debates can always be reduced to citations from the Holy Scriptures, Lenin dixit, 'It is written in Marx.' " This is not the place to overhaul the inner significance of these intense acrimonious debates on the ideology of Communism. It is enough here to note that they recall the atmosphere of either the early councils of the church or the period in Protestantism of "the dissidence of dissent."

As a result of all this we discover as an integral element in the world campaigns of Communism the development of what we can almost call a community of saints, or in other words, the church. The Communist Party, composed solely of members of the proletariat class, with its rigid process of education by catechism and confirmation through the Komsomol, numbers a few million out of the hundred and sixty millions of people in the Union of Soviet Republics. This tiny minority elects as its official organ the Central Communist Council, possessing a real dictatorship that reproduces oddly the early Puritan model of "the rule of the saints." The Executive, the Central Bureau of Nine, con-

---

[2] *American Review*, October, 1933.

trols all parts of the U.S.S.R., a sixth of the planet, for Communists are in governmental power in every republic of the Union, and any decision of the Central Committee is binding on members of the Communist Party in all the federated republics.

How does this control by the "elect" function? The system of government of the Union of Socialist Soviet Republics is by Soviets. The word "Soviet" is another word for "council." This technique of government was adopted by Lenin after the 1905 attempted revolution, when he saw the workers and the soldiers automatically organizing themselves into groups. At heart it is the principle of governing through representatives from organized occupational groups. Thus you have the workers' Soviet, the soldiers' Soviet, and the peasants' Soviet.

"Soviet" has nothing to do with Communism; but under Bolshevism the proletariat only is permitted to be represented through Soviets. It could, however, be used as a tool by a monarchy or any form of government. In fact the structure of the government of Fascist Italy is based on occupational groups. The House of Lords is the one Soviet parallel in British government. Alongside this Soviet system in Russia is the Communist Party, admission to which is by rigorous test and probation through local Communist "cells" in this factory, that army unit, yonder village or that government office.

These "cells" are represented in district committees in the rural areas, and in ward and city committees in urban areas. They in turn create, report to and get orders from the Central Committee at Moscow elected every two years by the Communist Party Congress. All members of the Soviet Central Control are Communists and all in authority in each republican government are Communists. Therefore, the Communist Party controls the Soviet Government, but in theory any party could equally well rule through the Soviets.

We have turned aside to define this issue in order to show how the relatively small group of Communists holds its dictatorship over the masses, and holds that authority through its doctrinal orthodoxy and fervid loyalty to the faith, as revealed in the scriptures of Marx and Lenin. One has the feeling that Karl Marx unconsciously carried the Jewish conception of an elect people into his idealization of the proletariat. As Nicholas Berdyaev says: Marx's "theory of the proletariat is in no respect scientific, it is religious, messianic, mythic. It creates the myth of the proletariat-messiah, the sole class free from the original sin of exploitation, the elect people of God and the saviour of mankind, inheriting all the virtues." [3]

Marx's doctrine is true in the sense that there is a proletarian class robbed of its birthright, calling for liberation from its yoke. But that proletarian class is made up of human beings, blended, like all of us, of good and evil, of nobility and degradation, of wisdom and stupidity. To isolate or to elevate a class is a sin against the brotherhood of man. Communism commits that sin; but so does the present economic and social order. Bolshevism inverts the contemporary order; stands it on its head.

Jesus Christ, the supreme revolutionary, lays His axe at the root of the evil, in His revelation of the ideal order in the Family of God. Communism and Capitalism are both fatally ensnared in the drag-net of materialism. For this reason it is a criminal futility to attack Communism, or its

---

[3] *Le Christianisme et la Lutte des Classes* (Editions "Demain," 15 Rue du Four, Paris).

present executive experiment of Bolshevism, unless we are prepared to adventure with equal and indeed greater courage on the Christian revolution.

Our analysis of the faith of Communism reveals the measure in which much that is central to its aim is entirely congruous with Christianity. As between a competitive and a cooperative world-order every syllable of the Sermon on the Mount and every action of Christ pronounce for co-operation. Bolshevism is the greatest challenge to Christianity that has emerged in the world since the birth of Mohammedanism—and it has broken in upon humanity for the same reason that Islam did—because the Christian community was untrue to its essential task. There is a profound and prophetic challenge in the words of Nicholas Berdyaev that: "The one thing to pit against integral Communism, materialistic Communism, is integral Christianity. . . . The whole future of Christian societies depends on whether Christianity, or rather Christians, decisively leave off supporting capitalism and social injustice: or whether the Christian world sets to work, in the name of God and of Christ, to put into practice that justice which the Communists are now introducing in the name of a godless collectivity, an earthly paradise."

This does not mean that the modern man in the Christian community must shape his individual life and his collective activity on the basis of analogy to Communism. Undoubtedly, much of the authentic appeal of Communism to the youth across the world lies in the fact that, in spite of the absolute falsity of its bleak materialist dogmatism, it is attempting tasks not only congruous with, but integral to the teachings of Christ and the Kingdom of God. The ideal goal and the practical action of the individual Christian

45

and the church in the world must spring, however, not out of any hatred of the basis of Communism or imitation of its program, but out of their loyalty to and communion with God in Christ.

How many millions of Christians every Sunday repeat, "I believe in God, the Father Almighty"? That really means a far more powerful sense of destiny and a more dynamic faith that the forces of the universe are with us than does the Marxian creed, "I believe in economic determinism." But does it thrill us with the same tremendous driving force? Does it fire us with the same faith?

We say that we believe in the Kingdom of God, but do we act upon it with the same realism with which the Communist acts on his belief in the planned, cooperative, classless society of world-workers? Could any ten thousand Christian boys and girls anywhere declare with ringing conviction "We are changing the world"? Do we really believe that in Christ the ultimate reality of the universe has broken through into time in conquering terms? Do we discover in the Incarnation the supreme triumph of the spiritual and the moral over the material order? Are we ready to give our life for Christ's standard of values? Do we even know what they are?

Have we not jumbled them up with a muddled heritage of contradictions, such as the Stoic view of property, the Roman sense of dominance, the industrial revolution's conception of success, and the mechanistic pattern of progress? Is not our first task the rediscovery of "integral Christianity"? And shall we not discover it as much through adventurous initiative as through intellectual quest?

The Christian salvation is a more revolutionary one than that of Communism. It means being saved from one's own personal futility within a divided personality into oneness and freedom and friendship. It is salvation from solitude in a bleak universe of self-absorbed mankind and impersonal nature into power and into fellowship. For the community it means being saved from internal antagonisms, from conflicting goals, from the materialistic tyrannies that are today driving mankind blinded through increasing chaos toward indescribable disaster.

The unity of man is fatally threatened by two equally atrocious demoniac conflicts—the wars of class and of nationality. The "home-base" of those great corporate sins is in Western civilization, the area where the Christian church has been dominant for so many centuries. Is the church fatally involved in them? Or can she shake herself free? Christianity does not deny the reality of the class-war or of the wars of nations, any more than it denies any other deadly sin. Indeed it is the supreme splendor of Christianity that it refuses to burke reality by the doctrine of illusion and the way of escape proclaimed by Hinduism and Buddhism, but realistically recognizing evil claims to transform it by new birth.

The class-war is there; it is real. Karl Marx has rendered humanity a great service by bringing that irrefutable fact into the foreground. Communism says fight to end the class-war by creating the dictatorship of one class, issuing in the destruction of all others. Class-war is thus ended because the proletariat becomes humanity. What does Christianity say? It says that Communism is, in the last analysis, rooted in an ultimate lie about the universe, the falsehood that the supreme and final reality is in economic forces.

Christ says, on the contrary, that the ultimate and the immediate Reality is God, that we are His family; that the goal of human society therefore is brotherhood. Christianity is in essence more communist than Communism because it is of its nature to share both the material goods of the visible world and the invisible treasure of the spiritual world. It is therefore in the name of God that Christianity condemns equally the present social order and the dictatorship of the proletariat, and above all the perilous compromise with materialism in which the church has so heavily involved herself. The menace to Christianity does not lie in a militant Communism, but in a recumbent church.

If, however, Christianity really means the brotherhood of man as the corollary of the Fatherhood of God there lies ahead of the Christian community in the world either betrayal of Christ or the great adventure of realizing that brotherhood in concrete reality, face to face with the harsh antagonisms of class, nation and race. The church, indeed, has within her own household all those antagonisms. In every part of the Americas, Europe and Asia, as in Africa, she confronts, within and without, the sin of class-discrimination, of race-antagonism, of nationalistic selfishness. How can she wage implacable war upon these sins if she is not herself free from them? There is no short or easy way through that dilemma.

The path is that of repentance and rebirth. Those within the Christian community on whose hearts this is the great concern must take the way of sacrifice. They must come to the foot of the cross. They must share with their fellows in all places and at all times the reality of the love of God that in Christ broke triumphantly in upon the human scene; and the hope through His body, the Christian church, of the realization of that brotherhood. They must, cost what it may, dedicate their individual lives, as well as the corporate life of the church, to that end.

To attempt a definition of the essentials in the social program of Christianity in face of this crisis requires the collaboration of the finest Christian economic minds in the world. Such an adventure is long overdue. "The Findings" of the Jerusalem meeting of the International Missionary Council in 1928 with regard to the world mission of Christianity in relation to industry incorporate a piece of notable world leadership.

They sound the most advanced note yet struck by world Christian forces and are most significant in that they express the voice of the church in every continent. Something is urgently required, however, that is at once more prophetic and more scientific than any group with a general world background is able to present. R. H. Tawney, Bishop McConnell, Nicholas Berdyaev and others are making creative individual attacks upon the problem. Will other scientific and adventurous economic Christian experts not now join them and give world-Christianity a new lead in this most needy area?

Pending such a lead, there are, however, surely certain applications of Christian principles that give guidance. First, no Christian can desire to buttress the passing order. We could not if we would; but we would not if we could. That order possesses some eternal values that must be conserved; but, in the main, it has been weighed and found wanting. It is ethically and economically bankrupt. Even on a purely scientific basis economic individualism or nationalism in an interdependent world is lunatic. On any moral basis it is criminal. For a Christian, secondly, the founda-

49

tion principle is to move with all possible speed from this acquisitive to a cooperative society. To this end, thirdly, he must fight for the integration of cooperation into every element of industry, cooperation rooted in goodwill and aiming at the common welfare. This involves, fourthly, subordinating the acquisition of raw materials, manufacture and distribution to social aims and, so far as is called for in view of those aims, to social control. The horizon of those social aims, fifthly, is neither civic, national nor racial, nor that of any class, but is human on a world scale; and even human welfare is to be regarded, not from the purely physical point of view, but from that of the total manhood as cherished in the mind of God. Labor, sixthly, should suffer no inequalities of reward for its work that have no final economic validity, and should shoulder its full share of responsibility within the economic and social structure.

If those principles spring direct from a Christian ethic they give us something to go on with in the way of transforming the present order. If critics hold that they do not come from a Christian ethic it is high time that the experts show us what practical program does spring up from that ethic. For an absence of creative initiative by Christians in the present economic world crisis would be a major tragedy. The church is in peril of abdicating from her supreme function as the divine saving leaven in the world. We need the engineer's blueprints of the Christian economic world revolution. It is not at all a question of the church taking sides with or against any class. Her concern is with man, and with man as a Person—an eternal being, a Son of God. That is, indeed, the glory of Christianity and it raises the church—if she is true to her Lord—into a position dominating Communism and Capitalism, mechanism and imperialism.

For they deal with man impersonally. And they do so not by accident but inevitably. It is of the essence of Christianity to see man as person, and as person because he is a member of the one eternal community, the Family of God.

Christians are in possession of something far more revolutionary than Communism. For Communism is essentially reactionary and conservative.

Communism, when it has achieved economic material comfort in a classless society of comfortable, well-fed, well-clothed, well-housed people on a world scale will, if Marx's economic doctrine is true, have reached its goal. The Communist society, when once achieved, will therefore be static, conservative, less progressive than any civilization even India or China had ever seen. The imagination staggers in an attempt to conceive the illimitable boredom of the world Communistic state.

The goal of the Kingdom of God, on the contrary, is, by its very nature, eternally calling man across fresh horizons of achievement to ever higher plateaus of life. The call then to the modern Christian face to face with the faith of Communism is to an integral dedication to the project of the Kingdom of God. Confident in both the will and the power of an Almighty Father to achieve it, the Christian community is bound to give an absolute loyalty and sustained enthusiasm, and to accept joyfully an intellectual and moral as well as spiritual discipline adequate to building on earth the walls of that City of God whose plan is already laid up in the heart of the Father.

III.

THE NEW RELIGION OF NATIONALISM

THE meaning of any age is most clearly portrayed by its religious or semi-religious symbols. The value of the symbol or of the symbolic act as a commentary upon human society depends, of course, upon the extent to which it achieves universal acceptance, and its universality will in turn depend upon the degree to which it sums up and expresses the collective interests and desires, hopes and fears of the society which employs it.

Vast sections of the human race have packed their goods and have left the land of their fathers. We are in the midst of a gigantic trek of the human spirit, a trek whose significance is enhanced by the fact that it moves to the conquest of new societies rather than of new territories. In the vanguard of the marching columns go the symbols of the herd—like the battle flags before a Napoleonic army. To know what the symbols are and what they mean is to understand who the trekkers are, where they are going and what they intend to do when they get there.

What are the significant symbols of the Western world? What are the symbols that say most accurately what the people want said—that symbolize most perfectly the objectives which they wish to realize? Is it the Christian cross? It once was. It is so no longer. In the confused chaos which succeeded the collapse of Nineteenth Century civilization a multitude of new symbols have had their day. Many have disappeared among the debris, but some have survived and among the latter a few have earned the right to be regarded as typifying the most dynamic social forces of the coming age.

There is the hooked cross of Germany, the passionate violence of whose living symbolism relegates the Christian cross into the shadow as the ghost-like wan reminder of a dead but illustrious name. There is the statue of Italia with Mussolini kneeling in devotion before it. There are also the tombs. There is the eternal flame burning before the grave of the Unknown Soldier under the Arc de Triomphe in Paris. There is the tomb in the Red Square of Moscow; at once the tomb of Lenin and the temple of Communism, the shrine of the most powerful social faith that the world has ever known. These are all symbols. They are symbols of the world in which we live, and as such they furnish us with a kind of key to the mystery of its destiny.

What are the realities which these things symbolize? Above all and before all they symbolize the deification of the nation-state. They symbolize the birth of a new type of nation and a new kind of nationalism. The nationalism which they represent is utterly different from any nationalism which has existed hitherto. Even the most red-blooded patriot of the Eighteenth and Nineteenth Centuries seems rather anemic in comparison with Hitler.

The new nation-state is the exclusive social unit through which great masses of mankind expect to achieve their destiny. For its members it is not simply one society among many; it is *the* society. It is the all-inclusive collectivity which embraces and gives meaning to the total life of its members. The nation becomes an organism, and the organism functions through the legal and administrative framework of the totalitarian state. Thus the totalitarian state and the National Being enter upon a mystic union and are merged into a mystic whole, one and indissoluble.

The totalitarian nation-state asserts itself as the final object of loyalty for its citizens. It is the norm for personal and communal life. Nothing conditions it, but it conditions everything. Nothing judges it, but it judges everything. In the interest of maintaining its sovereignty over the mass of mankind it exploits the myth of a pure race composing the nation, of a pure national culture and of a pure national religion. Measures are taken to "coordinate" all phases of national life in terms of this myth. The nation-state so conceived becomes the be-all and end-all for its citizens. It is the supreme reality which creates all their standards and values. It is their social absolute and the object of their worship. In a word it is their God.

A pure form of the totalitarian nation-state cannot of course exist, though recent events in Germany illustrate how closely the ideal can be approximated. The significant fact is not the degree of approximation but the trend, and this trend, which amounts in some places to an avalanche, is universal. The Buy British mood of the Empire at Ottawa and Mr. Roosevelt's July 3 note to the 1933 World Economic Conference are but Anglo-Saxon expressions of the same forces which among the Germans have produced the more theatrical program of the Nazis.

Just as the characteristic movement of the Nineteenth Century was toward the liberal democratic pluralistic state, so the characteristic movement of the Twentieth Century is toward the unitary nation-state. Life after the World War became intolerable. People were ready for any change provided it gave the slightest promise of improvement. Democ-racy as a reasoned and ordered way of political life offered no hope of salvation. It was impotent because it had tol-erated and even encouraged the simultaneous existence with itself of an utterly undemocratic form of economic life. Democracy's alliance with Capitalism undermined the foun-dations of the democratic faith and destroyed its transform-ing power. Hence the devolution from democracy to some form of mass dictatorship became inevitable as soon as dic-tators appeared who could convince the mass that this would mean change and change for the better.

Heretofore states have been autocrats in action, oligarchies in action, or political parties within democracies in action in the presumed interest of the nation. But even during the democratic period of the last century the state was not conceived of as the whole nation in action. It has remained for our generation to identify the nation with the state. A Charles I or a Grand Monarch might have said, "The state, I am the state," but now the nation says, "The state, I am the state." As a result the nation-state is beginning to claim for itself all of the prerogatives which were once asserted by absolute sovereigns. On the pedestal which formerly sup-ported an idol named "the divine right of kings" we see a new idol being erected called "the divine right of nation-states." And the worship of this new idol is even more dan-gerous for humanity as a whole than the worship of the old idol.

The totalitarian nation-state is in some respects the most typical social product of modern civilization. Though its appearance at this particular juncture may be accounted for in part by the adjustments and maladjustments resulting from the World War, it would have appeared eventually even

55

if there had been no war. The tragic paradox of contemporary society is that it has stimulated man's hopes and desires far beyond his capacity to realize those hopes and desires within the framework of existing institutions.

Out of the tension between human craving and the failure of traditional social procedures to provide satisfaction for that craving the totalitarian nation-state has been born. It has promised a fulfilment which no other alternative offered. The masses became aware that under the existing régime there was continually less work, continually less bread and continually more insecurity. Individualistic democratic programs had been tried and found wanting; international programs were discarded before they had been even tried.

In so far as the choice lay between the dispassionate reasonable liberalism typified by Mr. Lippmann and the passionate irrational nationalism personified by Mr. Hitler the issue was never for a moment in doubt. Faced with such alternatives the masses will always make the same choice. And there is some reason in their madness.

In 1929 Mr. Lippmann wrote *A Preface to Morals* which served for a time as a kind of Aurelian *Meditations* for semi-religious American intellectuals. The closing sentences of this book give Mr. Lippmann's idea of a good man: "Since nothing gnawed at his vitals, neither doubt, nor ambition, nor frustration, nor fear, he would move easily through life. And so whether he saw the thing as comedy, or high tragedy, or plain farce, he would affirm that it is what it is, and that the wise man can enjoy it."

It was fortunate for Mr. Lippmann that he wrote this when he did. He probably could not have written it even then if he had lived in any less secure spot than New York during the age of prosperity. In a world whose financial and economic systems have completely broken down, where thirty million laborers are unemployed and where there are wars or threats of wars on every continent, to picture as the ideal man one who has nothing gnawing at his vitals and who moves easily through life smacks of spectatorial dilettantism. It is worse than that. The day will come when these phrases will be regarded as convincing evidence of the moral and intellectual bankruptcy of what was once thought to be the most promising section of the American liberal movement in the post-war world.

The blind and prejudiced instinct of the mass has been sound at least in this respect, it has ignored what had proved itself unworthy of trust. The only alternative left seemed to be the totalitarian nation-state, and it is in that direction that the mass is moving.

For more han two centuries the dominant social forces have been preparing the way for the appearance of such a society. The organization of modern industry has created the skeleton on which the body of the National Being has grown and in addition has supplied that body with organs and with arterial and nervous systems. Under the tutelage of the public school system the majority of people have attained a degree of semi-education which makes them peculiarly susceptible to mass suggestion. The press, the movies and the radio have been perfected to such an extent as instruments of propaganda that within a fairly wide range of possible reactions the persons who control these instruments can produce the reaction which they desire.

In other words for the first time in human history the factors exist which make it possible for vast masses of men to become conscious of their collective destiny, to affirm self-determination as the goal of their destiny, and to weld themselves into a compact phalanx united by a common will and inspired by a common devotion for the realization of that destiny. A hundred million people can now become suddenly articulate as a single social organism and can develop a political, economic and military strategy in relation to other similar organisms.

Such social regimentation introduces onto the human scene a political force of entirely unprecedented power. To the extent that this political force becomes identified with the totalitarian state and expresses itself exclusively through that state, peace between nations becomes a utopian dream. As long as such states exist human society will be recurrently reduced to shambles by successive wars, and if the Christian church is complaisant, it will rightly lose whatever spiritual and ethical authority it may have had over the minds of men.

It is therefore a matter of the greatest urgency that Christians should clarify the implications for the faith and for the church of the challenge presented by the totalitarian nation-state. We must become realists in the sense that we understand clearly the precise nature of the historic movements with which we have to deal, but realism is not enough. While continuing to make our analysis of the historic situation in which we find ourselves our primary duty is to use that analysis as an introduction to the assertion of the Christian message and the demonstration of the Christian alternative in relation to that situation.

From the standpoint of a Christian two aspects of the totalitarian nation-state present the gravest difficulties. One of these is the effect of this state upon the Christian's efforts to translate into human forms his belief in the eternal reality of the Family of God, and the other is the influence of this all-inclusive collectivity upon the integrity of personal life.

If the Christian's affirmation of the reality of the Family of God means anything at all it means his determination to work for a cooperative society of nations in which the standards of living of all nations will tend to approximate each other and where there will be institutions of a political, economic and legal nature which function to lessen the sense of national insecurity by providing increasing protection for the weak nations against the strong, and to secure for all a larger measure of justice in their mutual relation.

It has been only fourteen years since Mr. Wilson regarded the nationalism of his "self-determination" states as a necessary transition to sound internationalism. But between Mr. Wilson and Mr. Roosevelt there is a gulf fixed which no man can cross. During little more than a decade the concept of the state has completely changed. For Mr. Wilson the state was essentially the expression of the political life of the nation, whereas the economic life of the nation expressed itself through institutions and activities which were to a large extent independent of political control. He relied upon political self-determination to assure domestic social tranquillity, and by ignoring economic questions he trusted to the free play of economic forces in the world market to lay the social foundations of international political cooperation and peace.

Until 1927 it looked as though there was just a bare chance that his hopes might be realized. Since 1927 it has become increasingly obvious that the outlines of the world that is coming into being are utterly different from those which he anticipated. The really decisive war was not the armed conflict between nations during 1914-1918 but the titanic struggle for the mastery of the world that has been going on ever since between national economic forces and international economic forces.

The World Economic Conference at London is the latest battlefield, and in that battle international economic forces have suffered a crushing defeat. Economic nationalism has won because of its alliance with political nationalism. The moment the National Being asserted through the state its absolute sovereignty over the total life of the community the annihilation of international economic forces became inevitable.

The people are hungry for a Messiah, and the demagogues know that in the modern world the Messianic role can be played more effectively by the National Being than by anyone else. In comparison with the emotional responses which the Messianic nation-state is capable of eliciting and the loyalty it is capable of evoking, the emotions and loyalties aroused by the ideal of the world society seem like the gurgling of a mill stream in the presence of Victoria Falls.

The argument most frequently heard in defense of the Messianic role of the nation-state is that before the world can be cleaned up each nation must put its own house in order. Nothing could be sounder than to insist that national recovery is a condition of world-recovery, but the truth of this argument is twisted into a dangerous fallacy by the use of the word "before." In the world as it is today no nation can put its own house in order without at the same time cooperating in a common effort to put the world's house in order.

International action is futile without national action, and national action is futile without international action. The two do not represent separate spheres of existence with some people living in one sphere and other people living in the other sphere. There is but one sphere of life and it embraces both the nation and the world. International life and national life are but different aspects of one interdependent human society.

There are eminent economists at the present time who do not concur in this judgment. Dean Wallace Donham of Harvard thinks that nations whose nationals are engaged in international commerce are more likely to go to war than nations whose nationals preoccupy themselves exclusively with developing a home market. There is a certain measure of truth in this statement as an abstract proposition. But does Dean Donham really suppose that the citizens of the United States can become so completely infatuated with the alluring prospects of the American market supervised by the benevolent directors of the New Deal that they will forego all opportunities for foreign profit and actually stay at home?

The United States is obviously in a much better position than any other country to pursue a policy of economic nationalism because of the size of her internal continental market and because of the vast natural resources that lie within her frontiers. Given the kind of world in which we now live it is, however, perfectly quixotic to suppose that either the American government or the American people can be kept at home, whatever the vote-catching policy of any particular administration may be.

They will continue to go abroad and they will continue to compete more and more keenly with other governments and with other peoples in the world market. Hence, the attempt to base domestic and foreign policy upon a theory of economic nationalism rather than upon the actual facts of economic activity both at home and abroad is to court eventual disaster.

Supposing, however, that the idea were not quixotic and that commercial competition between nations could be effectively reduced to even a lower level than it is at present, the question still remains whether the situation resulting from that reduction would not in the long run be more favorable to war than to peace.

The current vogue of explaining everything that happens under the sun in terms of economic forces has perhaps been slightly overdone. Even if commercial competition between nations were eliminated, other international forces inimical to peace would remain, such as the pressure of excessive population, the discontent of strong racial minorities, land hunger, cultural contempt and race hatred. All of these forces have their economic aspects, but they cannot be considered essentially economic phenomena. If the danger of war is to be eliminated, nations will have to agree upon a procedure for dealing with such questions.

That means the establishment of the institutional outlines of a world society, and any government which permanently refuses to identify itself with efforts toward such an establishment under the excuse of the necessities of economic nationalism has doubly betrayed its citizens. It has betrayed them by giving them a false picture of the relationship between national and international life, and it has betrayed them by its talk of peace when war is the inevitable logic of the policy upon which it operates.

For in the last analysis the issue of peace or war is not exclusively an economic question or a political question. It is also a moral question. Men fight because of their pride, dishonestly and greed as well as because of the maladjustment of economic forces, and this is as true of nations as it is of persons. It is the business of a Christian to try to understand the true character of the economic factors which furnish the raw material out of which a more ethical society will have to be built. But the final judgment which the Christian passes upon the totalitarian nation-state is not an economic judgment, it is a moral judgment. He knows that the triumph of that state will cast a terrible moral blight over the minds and souls of men.

Buy British soon comes to mean British is Best. The ideal of American self-sufficiency and self-containment soon comes to mean that only American things are A-one. In every country the National Being will tend to become narrow-minded, provincial and self-satisfied. Its ego will expand because it has ceased to have normal commercial and financial intercourse with other national egos, and such intercourse is essential if nations are to maintain a sense of proportion and recognize the implications of their being segments of a much wider community.

Nations like persons can become ethical only "in relationship." A world of national egos expanding in isolation is essentially an immoral world, and sooner or later the god of war, who is the incarnation of all immoralities, will take charge and conduct humanity to the arena in which these national egos, like bloated monsters, will put on a spectacle of the latest scientific technique and the most brilliant administrative skill in organizing mass slaughter as an edifying expression of the inner meaning of modern civilization.

The Christian brands the totalitarian nation-state as immoral because it represents the absolute denial of his belief in the Family of God. Instead of helping men to become neighbors it forces them to become gladiators. The Christian community and the totalitarian state represent permanently irreconcilable social loyalties.

The second difficulty which the totalitarian state presents to the Christian is its threat to the integrity of personal life. It is obvious that capitalistic individualism is both unethical in itself and inimical to the public good. But in rejecting individualism some countries have adopted the alternative of imposing a collectivism which practically obliterates the meaning of personal life. One evil has been exchanged for another. The fallacy of both individualism and collectivism is the same. Each concerns itself with one-half of human life and completely ignores the other half.

The value of a society depends very largely upon its success in taking into account the whole range of authentic human experience. As far as our time is concerned that means a form of society which recognizes a distinction between personal life and impersonal social forces. There should be public control of all impersonal economic and financial systems, but that control should be limited by the fact that the most intelligent and beautiful forms of personal life cannot be created without an opportunity for self-control. By personal self-control I mean self-control in a conscious relationship to other persons, and this is a very different thing from individualistic self-control.

The liberal democratic idea of liberty was freedom from restraint. The Christian idea of liberty is positive responsibility—not imposed from above but accepted in a position of relationship. So far as the totalitarian state refuses to recognize a realm of personal life in which personal responsibility can be cultivated and insists on the imposition of authority from above over the whole of life whether personal or impersonal, to that extent again its life is completely anti-thetical to the life of the Christian community. It denies the Christian view of man, and by destroying the integrity of personal life denies to the person the possibilitiy of becoming a son of God.

The triumph of the totalitarian nation-state means that the Christian community is entering once more upon a period of severe testing. It is the ancient issue between God and Cæsar with this difference, that the issue is being raised now in a more critical form than at any other period in the history of the church. Powerul as Cæsar was, the absolute nation-state is an even more formidable opponent.

The will of a divine Cæsar could be avoided or circumvented or nullified far more easily than the will of a deified nation-state, since the latter is capable of achieving an omnipresence and omniscience which was utterly unattainable by the sovereigns of the Roman world. The difference between the threat of a Cæsar and the threat of a totalitarian state is the difference between the danger of being struck by lightning if one were in an exposed place during a thunderstorm, and the danger of being drowned if one were thrown into the middle of the Atlantic Ocean. The first is barely possible, the second is absolutely inevitable.

The central issue now is, of course, the same as the issue in the first centuries. Has the Christian citizen any existence apart from his existence as a citizen of the state? Will he burn incense to Cæsar or not? If not, what alternative does he advance and how does he propose to make that alternative effective?

The contemporary Christian attitude toward the state has been developed during a period when the state was waning in influence. After the church had asserted its freedom from the state it was generally assumed that the church would no longer suffer from political coercion. The political and social developments of the modern world prior to 1914 seemed clearly to indicate the approach of a time when such questions as the question of sovereignty and the question of authority would be largely academic. Consequently the majority of Christians are completely unprepared for the conflict which has suddenly broken upon them. Neither in their theory of society nor in their theory of the church nor in their experience of Christian action have they the equipment necessary for the struggle which lies ahead.

There have been moments in the history of the church when she was not only prepared for this particular conflict but when she more than held her own in it. During the middle ages the spiritual authority of the church was such that she was able time and time again to assert the reality of Christendom over against the claims of the princes of this world. At Canossa it was Cæsar and not the Bishop of Rome who waited in the snow and bowed the knee. But the Christian community in the Twentieth Century has no agency comparable to the Vatican or the Church Council through which it can make its authority articulate.

The Protestant community as it exists today depends upon three forces to oppose the absolutism of the totalitarian state. There is first the force of the individual conscience, second the force of the national churches and denominations and third the force of an aroused public opinion. It is obvious, for instance, that each of these forces has in its own way played a part in moderating the aggressive violence of Hitler's program. Groups within the national churches of Germany are for the time being stoutly defending their freedom in spiritual matters. It seems certain, however, that in the end of the day none of these forces will be able to prevent the nation-state from achieving a considerable measure of success in asserting its absolute authority over the minds and consciences of its citizens.

Forces that were adequate to preserve spiritual freedom in the age of liberal democracies cannot preserve that freedom in the age of the totalitarian state. The individual conscience is ineffective because it opposes a purely individual and hence relatively feeble force to the most powerful of all social forces. The national denomination or church is on the whole impotent because the nature of its constitution makes it uniquely sensitive to the pressure of nationalistic forces. And finally an aroused public opinion obviously cannot be relied upon in a crisis to preserve the spiritual and ethical integrity of the Christian community.

It is perfectly true that an aroused public opinion may temporarily check and even modify the policies of a totalitarian state when that state exists in another country, but if it is the country in which the totalitarian state exists which is being considered, public opinion within that country will of course be the opinion of the dominant group and hence will support rather than challenge the absolutism of the state. The opinion of the Christian community in that country will, on the other hand, be the opinion of a minority movement and hence at many points will be diametrically opposed to the dominant public opinion.

Neither the individual conscience nor denominations organized along national lines nor an aroused public opinion can successfully resist the pretensions of the totalitarian state. Neither reason nor logic nor idealism can long withstand its advance. There is one power and one power alone that can meet it and deal with it, and that is the power of the Church

Universal—the power and authority of the world-wide community of believing Christians. That community exists, but it does not have adequate organs through which it can become articulate. As a social organism it is very largely both blind and dumb. It is the business of our generation to provide this community with the organs necessary for the effective expression of its spiritual and ethical power.

To put the matter in another way the social loyalty demanded by the totalitarian state can be modified only by the demands of another social loyalty, which transcends and conditions loyalty to that state. Individuals and ideas are helpless in the presence of dynamic social movements. The only effective opponent of one social force is another social force. The only force strong enough to overcome one form of collectivism is a higher form of collectivism. Therefore the absolutism of the nation can only be modified by a trans-national society. The Christian answer to the sovereign claims of a national organic society must be given in terms of membership in another organic society—the church —which conditions all other social loyalties.

What is the duty of the Christian in the presence of this situation? His first duty is to understand the Christian teaching in relation to that situation. One of the basic assumptions of the Christian faith is its doctrine of two societies and of two citizenships. Perhaps the most perfect expression of this teaching is to be found in the Epistle to Diognetus written by an unknown author presumably in the Second Century:

"For Christians are not distinguished from the rest of mankind either in locality or in speech or in customs. For they dwell not somewhere in cities of their own, neither do they use some different language, nor practice an extraordinary kind of life. Nor again do they possess any invention discovered by any intelligence or study of ingenious men, nor are they masters of any human dogma as some are.

"But while they dwell in cities of Greeks and barbarians as the lot of each is cast, and follow the native customs in dress and food and the other arrangements of life, yet the constitution of their own citizenship, which they set forth, is marvelous, and confessedly contradicts expectation. They dwell in their own countries, but only as sojourners; they bear their share in all things as citizens, and they endure all hardships as strangers. Every foreign country is a fatherland to them, and every fatherland is foreign. They marry like all other men and they beget children; but they do not cast away their offspring. They have their meals in common, but not their wives. They find themselves in the flesh, and yet they live not after the flesh.

"Their existence is on earth, but their citizenship is in heaven. They obey the established laws, and they surpass the laws in their own lives. They love all men, and they are persecuted by all. They are ignored, and yet they are condemned. They are put to death, and yet they are endowed with life. They are in beggary, and yet they make many rich. They are in want of all things, and yet they abound in all things.

"They are dishonored, and yet they are glorified in their dishonor. They are evil spoken of, and yet they are vindicated. They are reviled, and they bless; they are insulted, and they respect. Doing good they are punished as evildoers; being punished they rejoice, as if they were thereby quickened by life. War is waged against them as aliens by the Jews, and persecution is carried on against them by the Greeks, and yet those that hate them cannot tell the reason of their hostility.

"In a word, what the soul is in the body, this the Christians are in the world. The soul is spread through all the members of the body, and Christians through the diverse cities of the world. The soul hath its abode in the body, and yet it is not of the body. So Christians have their abode in the world, and yet they are not of the world."

The heavenly citizenship to which this Epistle refers is symbolized by membership in the church. The church is the agency by which the cities of this world are to be transformed into the City of God. Membership in the church is the organic social relationship which conditions, qualifies and judges all other social relationships. I am a citizen of the State of Virginia and of the United States and as such I have certain definite duties to perform, but I am also a member of another society whose frontiers are not the same as the frontiers of American society. It is this consciousness of a simultaneous existence in two worlds which constitutes the essence of the Chrisitan ethic. It is out of the tension between these two worlds that Christian action arises. There is the cross, there is the resurrection, and there is the passage from death into creative and eternal life.

If this is a true statement of one of the basic assumptions of the Christian faith it ought to mean for Americans that they are at one and the same time members of two societies, of the United States and of the Universal Christian Community of Faith. But in actual practice we are really members of only one society. We are American Christians; we are members of national churches organized within the United States and hence our consciousness of participation in the life of the Church Universal is neither particularly vivid nor continuous. We believe in the Church Universal as an ideal, we hope that the church invisible may some day become visible, but this belief and hope remain more or less in the realm of utopian dreams.

What is true of us is true of Protestants generally. The Protestant churches everywhere are in a desperately weak position to defend the freedom of their faith against the encroachments of political power. In the light of their actual situation it is obvious that a utopian dream of the Church Universal will never save them from being absorbed into the absolutist state. They will only be saved as they lose themselves in the actual living reality of the Church Universal rather than in a dream of that reality. The actualization in concrete social form of that Church is their sole guarantee against international anarchy on the one hand and personal enslavement on the other hand.

If the call of the latter years of the Nineteenth Century was "to evangelize the world in this generation" the call of these middle years of the Twentieth Century is to build once more the Body of Christ in human form, to incarnate in social movements and institutions the eternal reality of the Church Universal. The challenge that comes to us is to create a consciousness of that Church, to work on its strategy, to affirm its message and to establish the agencies through which it may speak and act. The Christ lives, but men have failed to provide the Living Christ with the Body through which He may do His redemptive work.

A world-wide community of faith exists, but its members

are for the most part not conscious of its existence. This community is implicit in our faith and in the fellowship of our churches. It needs to be made explicit. The task of our generation is to give to the Community of Faith a consciousness of its existence, to put meaning into its membership and to provide channels through which it may function more continuously and effectively.

This task cannot be achieved by either of the alternatives that most readily occur to a Western Christian. Our Protestant tradition has accustomed us to expect either of two possible procedures when men become convinced of the necessity for a new departure in Christian thought and action. We expect either the formation of a new sect which claims for itself the honor of being the chosen remnant, or the inauguration of an ambitious world-shaking program of activity. As we know all too well from experience the adoption of these alternatives would be fatal.

There is a third possibility which is that those to whom this conviction comes would, each in his own station, form the habit of thinking and acting in the interest of the Church Universal. In the course of time persons who did this would by the logic of their assumptions be forced to associate together in groups for the purpose of corporate study, demonstration and action. Out of these groups a world-wide interconfessional movement might eventually appear whose life would profoundly affect the character of the existing churches and which would help to prepare the way for their finding their respective places in the larger fellowship of the Church Universal.

The appearance of the Church Universal does not await either a catastrophic apocalyptic event or the birth of an organizational genius. It comes into being now for those who really believe in its coming and who live under the inspiration and discipline of this expectation. It comes to all those who in their respective positions of responsibility enter into relationships which transcend sect and race and nation and culture because they incarnate in dynamic forms of corporate life the eternal reality of its spiritual and ethical communion.

A movement which fully symbolized the Communion of the Church Universal would possess the following characteristics:

Its life would flow out from the main stream of historic Christianity.

It would be more Catholic than Protestant in the sense that its members would be more interested in pooling all available resources than in differentiating their respective positions by dissent from others.

It would have a message of salvation for both personal and social life.

It would be Christo-centric in its belief in the Living Christ who is present wherever two or three are gathered together in His name.

IV.

THE WORLD ECONOMIC CRISIS

IT IS commonly asserted today that the economic forces in that part of the world called Christendom have solved the problem of producing enough material goods to prevent the race from starving, and that whatever faults there are in Occidental economic systems have to do with distribution and not with production. Very few defenders of the present-day system would care to declare that the distributive phase of that system is anywhere near what it ought to be. Capitalism, however, is supposed to have pointed the way toward such handling of the earth's resources as will yield enough return to satisfy the necessities of all men.

The defenders of the productive power of the present economic systems are taking it too easy in all this. Looking at the whole world, the current distress which we call the period of depression gives the West an inkling of what has been going on in practically all the other parts of the world since the beginning of time. The fault in the West has been due to the breakdown of the distributive system, but the starvation thus made imminent has been a feature of Oriental existence ages without number.

In Oriental lands there have not been enough goods to go round. Perhaps it would not be too much to say that, counting all men together, the majority of human beings on the earth at any particular date have not lain down to rest at any night-time having known through the previous twenty-four hours the satisfaction of enough to eat. It is but right that the men of the Western world should protest against the forces which have brought about our unemployment situation, but we are making a huge to-do over sufferings which have been common to the vast majority of human beings since human beings began to be.

Of course the advocate of our Western economic system will have it that the way to increase the productivity of Oriental lands is to introduce Capitalism to those lands. Before we accept this ready suggestion, however, let us look at some of the less material factors, especially in Oriental lands, which affect the effectiveness of material factors. Christianity must give itself more and more to the direct teaching that it is a Christian duty to increase the material responsiveness of the earth.

If the teaching of Jesus assigns so important a place to the giving a crust of bread to a hungry man as to make such giving a test of final judgment as to worth in the Kingdom of Heaven, surely the attempt to give men enough bread to do away with hunger altogether as gnawing pain, ought to be assigned an ever higher place. Christianity is on firm ground in teaching this direct responsibility for the larger responsiveness of the earth.

The peculiar sphere, however, in which Christianity is most responsible is that of the ideas which lie back of so-called economic forces and that of the ideas to which those forces give rise. It may be that those students are right who tell us that man was at the beginning completely at the mercy of the material forces in which he found himself, and that his ideas of himself and his world were the direct result and outcome of the physical surroundings of his existence. It is a peculiarity of ideas, however, to persist long after the forces which first produced or occasioned them have ceased to work. They persist out of sheer human inertia, if for no other reason—out of psychological slowness—out of habit—out of social and individual conservatism. So it happens that economic activities, which at the outset had a value in aiding men so to adjust themselves to the world as to win a livelihood from it, arrive at the end at forms of material waste and maladjustment.

Quite a thesis could be written on the economic wastefulness of false or inadequate or antiquated views of the world and life. China and India have together nearly, if not quite, half the total population of the earth. In China one of the most potent of all beliefs is that in ancestor-worship. It is estimated by students as careful as Professor E. A. Ross that the demand of the Chinese social and religious systems for sons to care for ancestors is responsible for one and a fourth times as large a population at a given time as would be likely in a land which did not believe in ancestor-worship.

Now it may be altogether possible that ancestor-worship began in China—or increased to large results in China—because of the economic need of having large masses of labor-supply in an era when man-power was virtually the only power. The belief once in force has continued to flourish, and has under it all manner of social and psychological supports. If it be said that Christianity has no right to enter the domain of economic discussion as such, the reply is pertinent that Christianity is concerned with human values as such and that ancestor-worship bears directly on those values.

We may concede all reasonable force to the worth of belief in duty to ancestors as a spiritual factor, we may agree to the utmost that the Chinese ideal of the family to which ancestor-worship contributes is of vastly higher worth than the West has ever realized, and yet we must admit that where there are so many persons for such scanty food supply the worth of each person falls too low, that where the labor force is almost wholly man-force the man is judged almost wholly by what he can physically do, that the fact itself that there are so many laborers prevents the introduction of labor-saving machinery.

What is the use of saving labor if saving labor starves the laborer? It has been estimated that probably twenty per cent of China's labor is engaged in the various forms of transportation service. If, now, only half of this twenty per cent were to be thrown out of work by the quick introduction of railroads, the human cost would be inhuman. Moreover, the existence of such an immense reservoir of cheap labor offers every inducement to the outside nations—especially those of the West—to keep that labor supply intact.

The institution of caste also is today explained on economic grounds. With reasoning a bit obscure, the defenders of India's social system tell us that the economic adjustment of earlier peoples to Indian conditions made necessary the division of labor which later hardened into castes. I have never been quite able to follow the arguments which profess to explain just such subdivision of labor in India. Other races have met similar necessities without such hard-and-fast subdivisions.

Granting all conceivable force to the argument, however, it does not help us much to wave aside the difficulties presented by the Indian caste-system with the summary remark that the system originated in economic needs. The question today is whether it meets them without excessive human cost

—whether under the system the mass of human beings involved gets a chance at what might be called normal human life. Was untouchability, for example, a necessary and inevitable result of an economic demand? Is there any such resemblance of Indian caste to European syndicalism as some Indian thinkers profess to see?

It is sometimes declared by critics of Christianity that Christianity has no right to thrust its theology upon non-Christian peoples. This usually means that Christianity is engaged in teaching a Western scheme of theology, founded upon Western philosophy, to peoples who are not interested in formal theology. There does not seem to be any powerful demand for such theology just now either in the Occident or Orient. If there were any considerable attempt to put upon a non-Christian people a formal theology of any kind, Christian or other, there might be reason for complaint, though the situation created by such attempt in these days could hardly be called serious.

Formal theology to one side, however, we must recognize that every people has some view of man and his world whether we call it philosophy or not, and that these views bear directly upon the daily activities of the peoples who hold them. To take a single illustration, economic only in the broad sense of an influence affecting the welfare of a country's population, may I say that I once passed three days in an Indian village in time of cholera panic. The scientific workers who were struggling to abate the plague found their greatest obstacle in the idea of the villagers that cholera is caused by a cholera demon who can be frightened off by shoutings and the beatings of drums.

If we should choose to call this belief in demons a theology, we could find ample reason for doing so. All the

Christian teacher might be trying to do in his theology would be to cast out the theology about demons for the sake of getting accepted a more rational view of the universe, including the cause of cholera and the way to deal with it. Saying that the non-Christian peoples in the villages I visited should be left to their own theories of life and the world is saying that they should be left to their theories about cholera —which means that they should be left to cholera.

Max Weber has said somewhere that the reason the Jews came more quickly to commercial success than did their contemporaries of olden days was that the world-view of the Jews did not call for reliance upon auguries and omen-inspections and casting of lots before a trade could be carried through. The Jews did not have to examine the intestines of a chicken before concluding a deal. No matter whether our fathers formulated their views of the universe under the pressure of economic forces or not, they early reached a place where the theories thus formed were no longer adequate.

The larger, more rational ideas of man and the universe taught by Christianity certainly look in the direction of a more rational handling of the world in which men live. There comes a time in the development of any people when they add to the process of being adjusted to the forces of nature, that of adjusting those forces to their own requirements. This second process is very slow at first, as compared with the rapidity with which the changes take place later on when men feel themselves masters of a new force, such as electricity, let us say.

Still, it is possible here to fall into a double error—first, that of underestimating the extent of the earlier applications of a newly discovered power. Fire-making, once discovered, very likely passed soon into wide use. Second, to keep close to the idea I am trying to enforce, the ideas which are produced by an earlier stage of economic existence, or which grow up with that stage as harmonious with it, linger along into later stages.

Closely connected with the invention of material machines which influence economic activity is the making of laws which directly or indirectly relate to that activity. In a famous passage in the *Federalist,* James Madison allows it to be inferred that the builders of the United States Constitution recognized that economic forces must be ranked high among the factors to be taken account of in nation-building. It may be that Madison did not intend a single separately considered paragraph to be taken quite as seriously as students like Beard are taking it. Nevertheless, there is the utterance, revealing a deliberate recognition of the economic force and presumably an intention to deal with it—one of the first important statements of the need of recognizing such forces. It requires only the slightest familiarity with American history to realize the extent to which men of the school of Hamilton proposed to influence legislation to take advantage of and profit by economic forces.

Just at the moment there is increasing demand that there be deliberately planned economy on a world-wide scale for the sake of human welfare. Roscoe Pound has insisted that the bulk of American legal enactments were fashioned with rural conditions in mind, since there were no other considerable conditions until quite recently. The urban conception of life in this country came after urban conditions began to be common. There has been a most notable movement of late years to the city, but the ideas which ruled in other than city conditions are still prevalent. So that we have laws which came out of one type and view of life fitted by all manner of stretching on the one hand and pruning on the other. Christianity must face its task of contributing something to the ideas which help man's control over the earth on which he lives.

I have mentioned only the productivity side of economics —the need of getting more goods from the earth. I think that Christianity can make out a fair case for the claim that whatever tends to larger and better life for men tends toward a larger and better response of the earth in a general way, but I think Christianity has to face the problem a little more specifically and concretely than is usually done. Convinced as I am that the great material curse of the world is poverty, I think Christianity has to do more than just to rest with the statement that the preaching of a better ideal for man will lead to larger material wealth.

I have selected illustrations of the way that an inadequate view of the world in which men live will affect their effective handling of the earth from non-Christian nations. My reference to ancestor-worship and the belief in cholera demons may seem to put the non-Christian nations low in the scale of intelligence, but my knowledge of economic conditions would be indeed small if I did not see that just as absurd situations can be found in that type of Western civilization which prides itself most on its control of physical forces.

There is a somewhat general notion abroad in Western lands to the effect that the best thing that could be done for Oriental lands would be to introduce Western Capitalism outright. I do not know that this notion is as common at this immediate instant as it was before the present depression set in—or at least it is not as glibly uttered as ten years ago—but in spite of the depression the notion is common enough to take still the characteristic form of saying that the capitalistic weakness is only with distribution and not with production.

Now, if we are going to recommend Capitalism for the whole world, we must be careful to ask how its parts fit together. Can we get the most out of a system that is frankly faulty on the distributive side? What is the incentive to work if the economic scheme is so organized that the large share of the returns in dividends go to those who do not work? If it be said that if labor's share of the economic return is large enough to meet the laborer's needs he has no ground for complaint, it must be replied that the mere amount of goods paid to labor may not be the only vital consideration —that the differences between amounts for labor and amounts for owners may be so great as to create social and political differences as burdensome as actual lack of food and raiment and shelter.

Lord Olivier some years ago wrote a book entitled *White Capital and Colored Labor* in which he discussed the charge against colored labor that it was slovenly and lazy—that it would not produce beyond a certain low maximum. It is admittedly hard to fit this charge into consistency with the well-known fact that, in spite of their inefficiency, the masses of colored laborers are sought for the world over by employers. But let it be granted, for the sake of the argument, that colored labor is inefficient. Olivier asks what earthly reason there is for colored laborers being any more industrious than now with the lion's share of the return going to white capital?

So it is with the problem of capital and labor the world over. We are told that in the economic world we must think of the pursuit of wealth as a race between athletes. We shall look a little later at this claim that the economic life is a running race, but grant its force for the moment. A race—of all activities—must be absolutely fair if it is to command anybody's interest for long. No—we cannot divorce the distributive aspect of an economic system from the productive. If it is the duty of Christianity to stand for the increase of productivity, it is by the same token a duty to stand for such reorganization of the distributive aspect as will make distribution fairer than it ever yet has been. No one plan for such readjustment will meet the needs of all nations and groups—but whatever the plan, the aim should be clear.

Now someone, fascinated by the marvels of achievement of science in the economic field, tells us that at least machinery, in the Western meaning, should be introduced the world over if we are to get the returns from the earth in the amounts the world needs. It is hard to withhold agreement from this insistence. The invention of machinery has not only increased the productivity of the physical forces but has made definitely for the humanization of life. It has taken off men's shoulders burdens too heavy to be borne.

The progress of material civilization has consisted in large part of getting burdens out of men's hands and into the grasp of tools. In the beginning, almost the only way a laborer could handle a burden was to lift it and carry it. By degrees he learned the use of levers and wheels and finally the stupendous powers of the world as we now know them. There is a well-authenticated story of an old-time Haitian despot who, in supervising the transportation of huge blocks of stone up to a castle which he was building on a hilltop, gave orders that the bearers were to be shot if they showed signs of weakening. There was a time when the social organization, or lack of it, did about the same with workers who faltered. It did not kill them outright as they weakened under their loads, but it might just about as well have done so, as far as the ultimate outcome was concerned.

It can be said, too, for the advocate of machinery, that there are vast areas of the earth's surface over which men are borne down today by the sheer weight of physical burdens. Anyone who has ever listened through day after day to the creak of wheelbarrows in China, and has seen the strain on human muscle in pushing such barrows, realizes what hard labor is, labor, too, that could be relieved by the coming of machinery. Still, in China the laborer has made an adjustment, sanctioned by long centuries of labor custom, which relieves this strain. The laborer knows how to protect himself. He is the heir of all manner of understandings as to how to give a minimum of exertion, and get a maximum of relief. There are codes, not written indeed, but nevertheless inescapable and irresistible, which give the laborer something of an advantage in his daily struggle for livelihood— breathing-spells in the actual work and limitation of amount of work to be done in a given period.

This brings me to what seems an important consideration. In the exercise of that influence on public opinion, which is the outstanding task and opportunity of Christianity in relation to the larger social questions, stress should be laid on the creation of a social atmosphere which will supply the conditions under which masses of men can pass into a machine age. It is only gradually that we are coming to such control of machinery here in the United States. Many of the counts against a machine system are items to its credit. For example, quite enough has been made of the indictment that machine labor is monotonous. The farmer's life, which has been so often placed over against the factory worker's as being freer, has its monotonies. All work that can be standardized into regularity is monotonous.

It is mistaken to say also that society suffers from standardized processes as over against the artistic advantage of having every tailor and every bootmaker work the clothes or the shoes through from start to finish, with the idea and picture of an artistic whole before him. This is one of those commonly accepted deliverances which are dangerously near to being funny. Does anyone, whose memory goes back to that day when clothes and boots were made in the local shops, think of his various outfittings as masterpieces of art? No—the people of any Western land are more artistically and æsthetically clad today than were their fathers who were ministered to by the alleged talent for the beautiful of tailors and shoemakers.

The real trouble is more fundamental. The invention and use of machinery have outrun the development of a public sentiment that would keep machinery in its place. For a long time the people of the United States looked upon a railroad as just another public highway. In trying to bring railroads under social control, the public mind had to start from a gravel or "pike" road basis, and lingered along for a generation or two trying to fit a mechanism which was meant for increasing congestion of population to a scheme which had on it all the marks of rural individualism.

We have done somewhat better with the automobile. Yet here again the old notion that a man can drive as fast as he pleases on the public highway—a notion sound enough when a horse could not average more than six or eight miles an hour and a runaway could barely reach twenty—seems to lead some autoists to fancy they have a right to tear along at seventy miles an hour. Autos on the public highway cease to be menaces only when codes of rules develop which have the rigorous support of public sentiment—a sentiment which men will regard whether officials are at hand or not.

In the large it is so with all machine economics. The economic field considered as a race is dubious enough on any basis—and highly dubious when the racers are not individuals with hand-tools but corporations with all the high-powered enginery of modern science. We have not yet worked out the conditioning and controlling sentiment in the Occident for a machine type of civilization. What then the responsibility on him who urges such machine civilization where the rules of economic behavior are those of an economic activity which has existed almost unchanged for a thousand years?

Machines of any order are safest in the hands of the peoples in whose midst the machines have been conceived and built. I intend no disrespect to the Latin-Americans, for example, when I say that they are not traditionally of a mechanically minded type. The average Latin-American workman who learns to drive a car drives like Jehu. There is not back of him enough mechanical training in "feel" to make for any restraint whatever. So also is it when the Latin-American revolutionist is given high-powered machine guns, though here Europeans, who boast the height of their culture, handle explosives in war with a mentality which ought not to be entrusted with anything above bows and arrows.

As an illustration of what I mean by the introduction of machine organization into non-machine civilizations without taking with them the safeguards of Western industrial society, may I mention an incident which came under my own observation in China in 1922. A cotton mill in Shanghai introduced American machinery and stripped the machines of the safety devices used in America. Public sentiment—to say nothing of factory inspectors—would not tolerate such disregard of protection in the home land in which the machines were used by thousands of operators.

There are dangers enough to workers in China, but there is needed in China all the protection for workers which an alert public sentiment can build up against present-day machinery. In this particular instance the Chinese employers had to meet the demands for damages by the parents of a girl killed in a mill. The girl wore her hair in a braid after the Chinese fashion. The braid caught in the machinery and the girl was killed. The employers then made use of an out-of-date provision of American law and escaped payment of damage. They used the legal doctrine of contributory negligence and made the girl responsible for her own death.

We are forever hearing that in the industrial realm the Oriental nations need to adopt outright and at once the scientific method. Here again we do well to remember that the scientific method is safest in the lands that have wrought out that method. No matter how materialistic the Western nations may be, there lingers in the minds and deeds of the most materialistic scientists a sentiment, a feeling which is not materialistic. That sentiment keeps materialism itself within bounds that it might pass over if it were allowed to run loose in an atmosphere which would welcome materialistic theory outright and would proceed to the starkest materialistic activity.

The situation is not much better when the scientific materialism moves into an atmosphere without much considered thought of the worth of men as such. Socially speaking there is no better argument for Christian missionary effort than that which emphasizes the need of a substantially Christian view of man and the universe in the lands which are now taking over, or will soon take over, the scientific method as taught and used in the West. An atheist some time ago remarked to a group of friends that China needs above all else the scientific method—and then added: "Worked in the spirit of Jesus Christ."

All the high-powered productivity of Capitalism appears as a grim stupidity when that productivity runs so far and so wild that men by the millions are thrown out of work, and are deprived of access to the products which they are supposed to consume.

By this time it becomes apparent that society must be so organized that competition—even in the regulated form in which we now know it—must give way to something more closely cooperative. All that I have thus far said leads up to the conclusion that we have to look toward a planned society—and, if we are thus to plan, the ideas of human life peculiar to Christianity must be brought to the fore. The old days of speech about "enlightened self-interest" will not serve us here.

Of course, it was always possible in those earlier days to speak of the self as incorporating within itself other selves and thus reaching over from self-interest to interest in others. This, however, is merely befooling one's self with words. Enlightened self-interest is still self-interest, and self-interest reaches a point where there is no enlightening it. This does not mean deliberate wickedness. It means merely that there come clashes between the interests of self and the interests of the whole which cannot be solved from the individual point of view, while to the individual his point of view seems everything.

Cooperation in any intelligible sense today means large-scale planning. We are being forced to such cooperation just to get as much from the earth as we need, if for no other reason. Can a society of persons working together for the purpose of making the earth more productive get out of the earth more than those persons working against each other each for himself? Of course there are those who tell us that even if cooperation will not produce as much as competition, we ought still to cooperate because it is more worthy in itself to cooperate. I think, however, with the world as hungry as it is, we would better keep the practical results of cooperation in sight.

As a matter of economic fact, the competitive field today is quite limited. Do great corporations compete against one another? Not to the extent they once did. They join together to compete against the labor forces, just as those forces cooperate so as to prevent laborers' competing with labor. The contempt for the "scab" is due to the scab's willingness to compete against his fellows at all times and all places.

Now it is the duty of Christianity to help create the public opinion which makes possible cooperation even through a radical reorganization of society which does away with individual ownership and control of the great tools of production, no matter what label we paste on the social forms. Organized Chistianity can help mightily in this direction. It is a more and more integrated social body on its own account, with full right and increasing skill in collective utterance which can and should be prophetic.

It is too late to say that Christianity has no right to speak in this field. The question is not as to what Jesus said, or what our fathers said, or what the standards of previous generations were. The question is simply, What is best for human beings here and now, as far as their largest and fullest life is concerned? It makes not the slightest difference as to whether this is a break with the historic continuity of ecclesiastical activities or not. If it be objected that this obscures the position of the individual as the object of the church's attempt to save men, the blunt reply has to be that to raise the general level of mankind is to give the individuals a better chance at moral character and to make salvation in any rational sense easier of attainment, and to render individuals more worth saving on their own account.

Cooperation will not avail much if it does not reach out beyond national bounds and become international. Just at the moment there is a recrudescence, even in lands like England and the United States, to say nothing of Italy and Germany, of an emphasis on nationalism, with each nation living economically to itself and presumably keeping out of the way of the others, except in the non-economic contacts. This would, I suppose, be somewhat like the circles in which individuals meet for literary or scientific or artistic or social purposes, in which it is bad form for one member to show any interest in how another makes his livelihood.

In such circles individuals can keep out of the way of one another, but can nations keep out of the way of one another? Remember that the nations today have—almost all of them—to get access to supplies of raw materials beyond their own frontiers. If, now, there is not always to be war or, what is almost as bad, the rumor of war, there will have to be among the nations of the earth a cooperative plan of rationing of such materials—a rationing which Christianity can support as making for peace and as rational and feasible in itself.

Again, the increase of material resources for men may have to be attained in part by there being fewer men. There is no need of being shocked by the mention of the control of the size of population. The world has been giving itself to such control since time began—sometimes with the most horrible and cruel means—infanticide, for example. The more open minds speak freely of contraceptive measures, and the more diplomatic of the "higher standard of living," as likely to reduce the size of families, which can only mean that the higher the scale of living the less inclined are those enjoying that scale to have large families. This whole field is admittedly complex and difficult; for some nations, like some families, should have more members and some should have fewer; but Christianity certainly has the duty of preaching deliberateness and care in dealing with the size of the population of the earth. Even the preaching of rational self-control can have an effect on birth statistics.

Once more, Christianity has every right to keep uppermost the human values. This, however, is a vague term and Christian teachers would do well to make it as concrete as possible, welcoming especially the findings of experts in the study of human conditions. While it would be foolish and silly to declare that every man should be a producer in a physical sense, Christianity should preach with increasing force that anything which makes human values larger and finer in any way throughout society, makes also for larger and finer control over the earth on which man lives.

II.

THE CHRISTIAN MESSAGE

The Chapters of this section were prepared by

V.

THE GOSPEL AND OUR GENERATION

P ART of the crisis of religion today is that it lacks an adequate message for the times. It does not understand God,
it does not understand man, and it does not understand
the kind of time we are living in. It cannot understand
them, because, willing as it has been to be simply a department of life, one among others, it has, in common with our
whole generation, become surface or horizontally minded;
and neither God nor man can be understood by a type of
mentality which thinks that everything can be interpreted
in terms of origens and behavior. The dimension of
depth, whether above us or beneath us, has practically disappeared from thought. Most popular Christian preachers
and most writers on Christianity deal exclusively with the
secondary truths of the Christian religion. Meantime Christian faith has been eviscerated, Christian life has become
enervated, and a general despondency has set in.

But there is something more serious. It is obvious that in
the world in which we live only a very limited time is going
to be available for religion in which to find, formulate and
proclaim an adequate message. The highways witness the
mobilization at different points of an increasing number of
crusaders who say they have found and point the way to
action. The new note of authority falls sweetly on the ears

of perplexed men and women. The call to arms gives them the bracing they have felt the need of. Either religion sallies out of its sanctuaries on those highways, its advent on the road being heralded by luminous, authoritative words, by transformed lives and a clear call to a new crusade, or the hosts on those highways will eventually force a sacrilegious passage through the sanctuaries of religion—in which case God, as in the past, will raise up from the débris new "children unto Abraham."

I.

Every basic attitude toward life is the expression of an abysmal satisfaction or dissatisfaction. Systems of thoughts, whose intellectual architecture are a marvel of investigation. and logic, are rooted in an elemental like or dislike. That being so, it is vain for thinkers and investigators who are dealing with data which have emotional value to consider that they can proceed in accordance with a purely objective criterion. There is no such criterion where the human realm is dealt with, or any realm which is directly related to our ultimate sense of values. Philosophers, theologians, psychologists, sociologists, will draw diametrically opposite conclusions from the data which they study, if, perchance, their basic attitudes toward reality are opposite. This is inevitable and we may as well recognize it. Our vaunted objectivity in the spiritual realm is pure illusion, simply because all thought on human life is a reflection of what we are, of what we like and of what we regard as significant.

A passionate faith, which is the most creative of life attitudes, is least of all the product of rational activity. It is not an induction of the scientific mind; it is the response of personality in its concreteness and its wholeness to a value that absolutely satisfies. When Nietzsche was asked how he justified Zarathustra, that tremendous type of super-humanity, who incarnates the transvaluation of all values, his only reply was, "Because I like him." Zarathustra, the child of his fancy, satisfied him. Zarathustra met him, one noonday of his life. He became his only friend, one who stood beside him in his unutterable loneliness.

There is no more ultimate criterion of truth than that which satisfies one, but this something must continue to satisfy in the most opposite circumstances of life. It must satisfy in the light of new knowledge and in the shadow of fresh mystery. It must satisfy when one's face is flushed with dawn and when growing twilight casts its gloom over a furrowed brow. It must satisfy when friends acclaim and when friends forsake one. It must grow in intensity in the measure in which it is shared with others. It must be an element in the infinite satisfaction of God which holds the universe together. Philosophy's deepest problem—the problem it has not yet seriously faced—is a critique of satisfaction.

A religious message must needs spring out of the solitary depths of a heart in which a faith has been born. Such a faith may be shared by others, but in each case it is an intensely individual and personal thing. It must be something which I not merely have, but something which has me, which possesses me, which is the master light of my seeing and the soul of my doing, something without which I cannot understand myself nor be understood by others, something which is my very life. There can be no religious message which is not the message of the faith of some individual. The attempt to formulate a religious mesasge based on a study of religious experience in general, or of human need in general, is no message: it is a theory, a theology or a philosophy.

A message is a living word out of a living faith. The problem of the truth of a message is the same as the problem of satisfaction with the faith that inspires it. A message must be clearly the message of an individual, the one and only thing he has to say to his generation, something he must say in order to live and be himself. But to be valid for others it must also be God's message to that generation, the message which God gave him to deliver. Sometimes Paul spoke of his message as God's gospel, or Christ's gospel; sometimes as *"my"* gospel. He could only give to others what he had found in his own experience, and yet what he found in his experience was what God gave him, as it was also what mankind and his generation needed to hear. A true and adequate religious message must therefore be the message of an individual; it must be God's message; it must be God's message to a concrete existing situation.

The way is now clear for an advance into the heart of our subject.

II.

A religious message, whatever more it be, must be at least a lyric. What one thinks and says is but an echo of what one is, and that has a history. At its lowest, prophecy is autobiography. Someone comes to the soul and possesses it. A word sounds within which cannot be silenced. A man need be no prophet nor a prophet's son, but if he presumes to formulate a religious message, those who listen have a right to ask him, "How did you come by that word, what has it meant in your life and thought?" If he cannot answer, he is a pure theorist; he has no right to speak.

The principles I have laid down force me to do something

I intensely dislike. If racial and personal reserve had their way, I would start in with a positive impersonal statement of the Christian message, from which the lyrical accent would be missing. But I cannot. In the spiritual realm the purely impersonal is sterile. It is only personalized truth that is creative, only a word that has become flesh.

At the age of fourteen I passed through a profound spiritual crisis. For months before I had been oppressed by a sense of distance from God. I longed to come near Him and to know Him. Something happened, something which I could only describe then as I can only describe today, thirty years later, in the language of the Ephesian letter which became my favorite book in the Bible. "You who were dead hath He quickened. . . . In Christ Jesus you who sometimes were far off are made nigh through the blood of Christ."

The dividing gulf was bridged. God became a living, loving reality in my life. I talked to Him naturally. Everything became new to me. The woods and hills looked different and the ground had a fresh smell. The romance of the New Testament, especially the letters of Paul, caught my imagination. Dumas's "The Count of Monte Cristo" was laid aside half read as not nearly so thrilling. The center of my new life and faith and outlook was Jesus Christ. I was intoxicated of love for Him. My heart, thought and imagination were gripped by the phrase "in Christ Jesus"—the Christ in whom history and eternity, man and God, the Crucified and the Living One, were blended. I felt called to the service of Christ, with a sense of vocation which at times in my life since then has been the only thing I could be absolutely sure of. My religious life from that time to this has been Christocentric.

I began my Christian life with what some would call the

Pauline Christ. In my early days, singularly enough, until I went to Peru as a missionary in 1916, the writings of Paul and the Epistle to the Hebrews meant more to me than the Gospels. As I look back, my religious life was more incandescent during that period than it has been since, but my ethical sense was less sensitive then than now. The first sermon I ever preached in Spanish was from the word in the Epistle to the Hebrews, "Having, therefore, an High Priest over the house of God;—let us draw near." For me Jesus Christ was, above all else, the transcendent priestly intercessor.

Before long I realized that in my new environment, the terms God, Christ, religion were shot through with baleful content for the spirits who possessed most interest in human welfare. I heard one say, whom I greatly admired, "For me to say God is to experience a sensation of nausea in my mouth." "The Christ whom I like best is He who made the whip and drove the merchants out of the temple," said a brilliant Peruvian professor to me. I want a masculine Christ," he added. "It would seem as if God handed over politics to men and kept religion for Himself," wrote a famous Peruvian essayist, who was still alive when I arrived in Peru.

It was clear that if I were to do anything in an environment in which the best people were clamoring for social justice, indicting religion as they had known it before the bar of morality, it would be necessary for me to establish a more intimate contact between my transcendent High Priest and concrete conditions around me. It was at that time that there came into my possession a copy of Glover's book, *The Jesus of History*. Immediately the Synoptic Gospels and the historical figure of Jesus took on new meaning for me. I became engrossed in the study of His personality and teachings, especially the Parables and the Sermon on the Mount. I was now convinced that the view of Christ that South America most needed for its awakening was the Christ of the Whip and the Christ of the Mount. In an environment in which religion and ethics were unrelated in the thought of people, in which the name of Christ was shot through with associations which made it futile to descant on His unsearchable riches, in which the phrases "a poor Devil" and "a poor Christ" were used synonomously and applied to a useless, worthless, ill-fated human, it was necessary to show that the figure of Jesus had been travestied.

In those years I believed more about Christ and experienced more of His reality than I put into my message. I had the feeling that my audiences were not yet ready to appreciate or understand the full truth about Him. I said to myself, they must learn to know Him as law before they will appreciate Him as gospel. They must learn to respect and stand in spiritual awe of Christ before they will be ready to believe on Him. They must feel ethically convicted by the Man of Galilee before they can be led to faith in the Crucified and Risen One. It was the approach which that peculiar religious situation demanded, yet I realize now that I dealt at the time almost exclusively with the secondary truths of Christianity and was secretly afraid of the intellectual reproach of the cross.

I later came to feel the insufficiency of the approach through the Jesus of history. It tended to produce ethical but not religious fruits: it created religious interest, but not religious faith. A tension, moreover, had arisen in my own life. The living Christ had become less real to me than he once was, while a host of new problems presented themselves. The Road to Emmaus appeared to be the symbolic road of the Christian generation to which I belonged. I was one of a number of wayfarers who were bewildered, like Cleophas and his friend. We too had "trusted" that the Galilean would have redeemed Israel, but behold—a cross!

We were a broken-minded generation, without a worldview and without passion. The Jesus of history had not redeemed the world. The attempt to follow Him as a teacher of ethics and as a religious genius was producing an intolerable tension in the lives of many fine spirits whom I knew. They were becoming totally disheartened in the effort to be good and to do good. Jesus grew stranger and stranger to them. It was clear that "Lives of Christ," instead of being biographies, were really autobiographies of the biographers themselves. Nor could they be otherwise.

The teachings of Jesus could not be reduced to the literary sections, nor His portrait to the facets in which Harnack and his followers found the authentic Gospel and the authentic figure of the Teacher. Eschatological elements could not be eliminated by any legitimate critical procedure from the Gospel records. For the Jesus of history attributed to his person, not merely to his teachings, ultimate and cosmic significance. If he belonged merely to history, how could he escape the inexorable relativity of history, and what right could he have to claim for himself an unique and absolute place among religious teachers? His claim was justified or he was stark mad.

The Jesus of history and the Christ of Paul could not be kept apart. To attempt to separate them was to inject an impossible dualism into history, into Christianity and into Christian experience. The Jesus of history, if he belonged exclusively to the horizontal plane of history, could not save Christianity or the world. He could give an ethic tinged with emotion, but not a crusading faith; a philosophy of religion but not a religion. It was then I listened afresh to the "ought" of the other Wayfarer on the Emmaus Road, that divine "ought" with which he met human "thought." It was a fresh encounter with Christ. New light flashed upon the old Book and the face of the Nazarene. When afterward I recalled the encounter my heart too was glowing. New light had brought new warmth.

Paul of Tarsus, to whom I had owed so much, was clearly not the great falsifier of Christianity. He was the first who really understood Christianity. He was, in Unamuno's phrase, "The mystic discoverer of Jesus." I found myself thus by a sense of personal futility, by the spectacle of the futility of the so-called social Gospel, by a sense of the tragic loneliness and futility of our generation, with its this-world-mindedness, by the problems raised by a critical study of Christianity, and, I suppose, by a natural homing instinct, driven back into the strange new world of Paul into which I had awakened as a boy in my early teens. I found it lit up with new meaning. All the values of the historical Jesus which had become so precious to me I discovered there in Christ. I found the ethic of the Epistles was essentially the ethic of the Gospels. The heart of Christianity I saw to be not Christ's revelation of God, but God's revelation of Christ.

Schweitzer and Deissman, Barth and Unamuno, Kierkegaard and Dostoevsky, have helped me since to understand aspects and implications of the Christian Gospel. In these years, for the first time in twenty, that is since the influence of the Hegelian philosophy had set up a terrific conflict between my head and my heart, between my religious experience and my interpretation of religion, do I know the meaning of full spiritual freedom, of inner release both emotionally and intellectually. The last phase of the struggle on the intellectual side came when Kierkegaard broke the spell of Hegel and I began to think reality in a new dialectical rhythm.

How can I defend this attitude toward Christ which began in my boyhood? As Nietzsche did his attitude toward Zarathustra. "Because I like him." He satisfies me. When Nietzsche says "Let Superman live," I reply "Let Jesus reign." When he says, "Superman is the meaning of life," I say, "Jesus Christ is the meaning of life." Why do I say so? Basically because Christ has given my life a meaning and a purpose. So much so, that if one were obliged to believe as Nietzsche did that the universe had no meaning, I would calmly and decisively say, "Then let us give it a meaning. Let us appoint a master for a meaningless and orphan world." Whether Zarathustra or Christ—the Man-god or the God-man—is to be master of the world is the crucial question of our generation. As to which of the two the world really belongs, history and God will decide. In case of conflict with culture, or civilization or religion, I stand with Christ.

In sadness and gladness, when facing a difficulty, as after a defeat or victory, there arise instinctively to my lips the same words, "Lord Jesus." My Lord sets me the chief problem of thought to understand Him, the chief problem of conduct to be like Him; He assigns me my mission in life to make Him inescapable as the true ultimate satisfaction of every heart's craving.

III.

Were this testimony a purely individual affair, it would be sheer poetry and psychology. But I believe it to be much more, for should I ever be forced to believe that my personal testimony to Christ were not grounded upon God's testimony to Him, my faith would go. My whole nature craves objectivity. I could not maintain a faith which I did not believe to be founded in the nature of things. At this point I drop the lyrical note and the use of the first person, which are not altogether natural to me, and pass on to the objective treatment of the theme. Has God spoken in any such way regarding Himself, regarding man and the world as that it might be called His testimony? There is no question quite so momentous as this.

Time was, in the halcyon days of romanticism, when religious thinkers waxed eloquent concerning God's testimony in nature and in man. It now becomes increasingly difficult to find in either that "sure word of prophecy" which is objective and authoritative, and which the deepest heart of our generation seeks. The secret of nature becomes more and more inscrutable. Who can decipher her signals so as to say for certain that at the heart of her there is something, some one, that cares for man and makes for righteousness.

"Nature, poor step-dame, cannot slake my drouth!
Let her, if she would owe me
Drop yon blue bosom veil of sky and show me
The breasts o' her tenderness.
Never did any milk of hers once bless
My thirsting mouth."

The divinity of man is not so obvious as it was once held to be. We hesitate to speak of him as a godlike creature, as the supreme organ whereby the universe comes to full self-consciousness, as the crown and meaning of the cosmic process. What is man? "The earth has a skin. That skin is full of sores. One of these sores is called man," said Nietzsche. "Man is an unsuccessful experiment of nature," says a modern pessimist. In the abysmal chambers of human nature, beyond where the gaze of romantic idealism ever reached, Sodom and the Madonna lie together. So Dostoevsky said, and who like him unveiled the heart of man? We made man the measure of all things. We seated him on the vacant throne of the universe. We believed only in man.

Do we believe in man now? Do we think that cultured, Twentieth Century man is a truer organ of revelation than a savage? If individual human beings will pass muster, what about man in society? What about nations, which Hegel regarded as the determinations of deity? Read Reinhold Niebuhr's devastating realistic critique of socialized man in *Moral Man and Immoral Society* and ask whether it is easy to believe in progress and the speedy advent of the Kingdom of God through man. Man himself becomes uneasy. In the phrase of a German thinker, already quoted in an earlier chapter, "Man has become uncertain in his autonomy." He is not sure whether he ought any longer to assume sole responsibility for the universe.

But we were sure that in that loftiest expression of human nature called religion, we listened to the testimony of God. We have descanted about religious values, and we have advocated that all religions should form a solid entente against secularism. But religion as such is in crisis. The comparative study of religions and the psychological study of the religious consciousness in search of spiritual authority lead only to relativity and scepticism. They give no authoritative word, nothing upon which to base a faith. They know of no sure testimony of God.

It is not enough, moreover, for the historic religions to be preoccupied about spiritual values and to feel kindly and brotherly toward each other in their common affliction. Even should they succeed in conserving alive a sense of spiritual values against secularism, can they hold out against sacralism, that tendency to infuse religious values into concrete areas of life, which has produced the new religions of Nationalism and Communism? Is there at the heart of the historic religions, popular Christianity included, that conviction and passion which can meet successfully the competition of these new religions with any chance of surviving? What communism did to Russian orthodoxy and what nationalism threatens to do to German Protestantism, give us pause.

We must needs go beyond nature and beyond man. From the nether side of both comes the testimony of God. Out of those two books which separately are called Testaments and together the Bible, there breaks upon our ears the testimony needed to give a religious message objectivity and authority. Treated purely academically, the Bible becomes a collection of insoluble problems. But in the ears of those who know how to listen to it a consistent testimony sounds. One of the arts we need to recover in our time is the art of Bible reading. The Bible can only be read understandingly on the road of real life, by a man who has become a problem to himself and is desperately in earnest about finding his way.

"The Bible," said Kierkegaard, "is essentially a letter from God with our personal address on it." It is necessary that the reader of the Bible should allow himself to be questioned by the book. "Who art thou? Where art thou? What doest thou?" The man who takes these questions seriously, who will be satisfied with nothing less than knowing himself as God knows him, with standing in that place where God would put him, with doing what God wills him to do, will inevitably raise other questions which he will direct to the Bible. He will address a personal letter to God. His questions will be of no academic character, relating to the nature of God and religion, the nature of man and the object of human life in general. They will all be of an intensely concrete character, relating to his personal life and relationships, such, for example, as "Who art Thou, Lord? What am I before Thee, Lord? What must I do? Lord, be merciful unto me a sinner." Such a one will fathom the secret of the Bible.

> He shall have gifts, the gift that feels
>   The germ within the clod,
> And hears the whirring of the wheels
>   That turn the mills of God.
>
> The gift that sees with glance profound
>   The secret soul of things,
> And in the silence hears the noise
>   Of vast and viewless wings.
>
> The veil of Isis sevenfold
>   To him as gauze shall be,
> Where through, clear-eyed, he shall behold
>   The Ancient Mystery.

He shall understand what Paul means by the "mystery," the "open secret of God."

What is this open secret? "I believe in the Bible," said Luther, "because I believe in Christ." And he added with true insight, "The Bible is the crib in which Jesus Christ is laid." If you make the straw bedding your chief interest, you may find more than one thorn to make your fingers bleed. If the wooden frame becomes your absorbing study, you may discover in its texture dents and knots and the corpses of burrowing worms. But if you are in earnest about finding God and His will for your life, you will hear in the Bible the voice of God, and your concentrated gaze will fall upon the face of the Christ child.

In that face, and in the successive phases of the life into which the child grew, you will find the "wisdom of God in a mystery." You will believe in the Bible. You will know that it is indeed the Word of God, because it has become so to you. You will discover how the most characteristic trend of prophetic thinking before Christ is symbolized in the pointing finger of the Baptist, "Behold the Lamb of God," and how the apostolic thinking after Christ issued in the great Christian affirmation, "The testimony of Jesus is the spirit of prophecy." (Revelation 19:10.)

A brief digression becomes necessary at this point. The crucial issue of religious thought in Christendom today is not the acceptance or the rejection of this part or that part of the Biblical records, or of this or that idea contained in those records. It is rather the acceptance or rejection of the particular world-view which underlies the Bible as a whole. The soul of this issue, which becomes sharper and sharper, is not between the Bible and science, or between the Bible and historical criticism. The ascertained results of neither of these affect the central issue.

This issue has really nothing to do with either science or history, but with a world-view which is obliged by its assumptions to reject the conception of a special and absolute revelation of God in history. We are thus back into the region of ultimates, for that matter, into the realm of ultimate likes and dislikes, of satisfaction and dissatisfaction, which provide the germinal assumptions out of which world-views are born. That being so, the problem here is a philosophical one, and an adequate critique of satisfaction, as indicated earlier, must play a major part in the solution of it. Meantime, there are some people who, having found ultimate satisfaction in Christ, for life and for thought, are able to accept the philosophical assumptions underlying the New Testament world view, and feel themselves perfectly at home in this world of thought so strange to those who have a different attitude toward Christ.[1]

The message that comes out of the heart of the Bible, the soul of prophetic Christianity, is a testimony, the "testimony of Jesus." This "testimony" has a double significance in the thought of the New Testament. It means the testimony which Jesus gave to God, and the testimony which God gave to Jesus. These two are inextricably bound up together. For the Jesus of the New Testament record is a figure who transcends the antithesis which we have set up between the "Jesus of history" and the "Christ of faith," as his paradoxical personality transcends the antithesis between God and man.

Jesus Christ bore testimony to God. On the basis of direct insight into the nature of God and of intimate communion with God he testified to what God is. He made the

---

[1] See Emil Brunner: *The Word and the World* for a discussion of this subject.

moral nature of God the standard for the perfection of man.
By precept and example he testified to what men should
be in the light of God and under the leadership of God.

Certain aspects of Jesus' testimony to God need to be
set in high relief. Between the God of Jesus Christ and
the God of the Old Testament saints and prophets there is
no breach. In the experience and thought of Jesus appear
facets of testimony to God which do not appear together
nor in the same intensity in any single Old Testament
figure, but no facet in His dazzling testimony is entirely
new. In the deepest stratum of the Synoptic records flashes
that basic presupposition of the Christian world-view, the
true and effective transcendence of God.

Jesus testifies to the living God. He does not merely talk
about Him; He talks to Him, and says in an ecstatic thrill
of joy, "I praise Thee, O Father, Lord of heaven and
earth, for concealing this from the wise and learned and
revealing it to the simple minded." (St. Luke 10:21.
Moffatt's Translation.) For Jesus, God is God, man is
man, the world is the world. God is so much God that
nothing is impossible for Him, man is so much man that
he cannot fathom the great deeps of God. God reveals His
secret to man but not to mere man, even be he developed to
the nth degree of science and culture, but to simple-minded
people who being aware of the frontier where man's powers
of insight and achievement end, wait humbly upon God.

God, the all-powerful and the all-wise is the all-loving,
and the all-holy, too. He is no God far off and indifferent.
He is so interested in insignificant humans and their affairs
that, in the figure employed by Jesus, he numbers the hairs
on their heads, and will call to account the despiser or
destroyer of any true human value. In the flashing eye of

Jesus, whip in hand in the temple courts, surrounded by the vested interests of injustice and unreality, we see mirrored the holiness of God and catch a vision of ultimate justice. In the tearful eye of Jesus in the presence of broken, unpretentious, pleading men and women, we receive a glimpse of the love of God and sense the true quality of that mercy which we and our generation need to receive for ourselves and to dispense to others.

For Jesus, God alone can be an end in Himself. To do God's will is man's goal. Those who make this their aim are regarded by Jesus as blood kinsmen, his father and mother, his brothers and sisters in God. It cannot be too much insisted upon that for Him no merely human end, however worthy, should be absolutized and pursued as an end in itself. Nothing is more striking than to observe the number of things which He might have interested himself in and which many think He should have interested himself in. He could have become the leader of many a philanthropic, social, cultural, political movement in first century Palestine. But he did not. His particular sense of mission excluded absorption by any minor interest. He was conscious of having a very specific task to do in loyalty to God.

What is the bearing upon human life of Jesus' testimony to God? It is futile for any man to try to imitate His particular "way of life" when confronted with the necessity of choosing his vocation, as it is also futile to inject a First Century social environment and social conscience into the Twentieth. Yet there is something of momentous import in Jesus' testimony to God which we need to realize in our times. Human life cannot be guided fully by reference to mere general principles or general truths, even, paradoxically speaking, if these truths be the teachings of Jesus. Man must be related to the concrete will of God. Here opens up before us a much greater adventure than that of studying and applying to our lives and the lives of others a concrete body of teachings. God, the living God, guides men in the concreteness of human living, from His Word. There is a region beyond religion and beyond ethics in the current use of these terms, where man listens to the living Word of God for his own life and the life of his time.

To those men and women who are interested not merely in having a religious experience but in knowing and doing the will of God, not merely in serving their fellows but in leading their fellows to know and to serve God, Christ bequeaths his peace. This is a paradoxical peace, "peace like a river," like the flow of water in a river channel. The water is at peace because its bed is made; it shall inevitably reach its goal in the bosom of the sea. But it moves in constant tension, flowing over sunlit meadows, disappearing in murky caverns, plunging in foam across the cataract's brow.

The peace which Jesus gave his disciples as His most precious legacy, in the hours before Gethsemane and the cross, is, in Christian experience, mediated to men as part of the peace which He became. Repeating the words, "He is our peace" and deeply conscious that that peace is the unspeakable need of this hour, we pass into the second part of the testimony of Jesus, the testimony which God gave to Him.

IV.

We now stand before the inner shrine of Christianity. Paul and John lift the veil before our eyes. The testimony of experience and the testimony of Jesus move us to enter.

The interpreting Spirit within unfolds to us the sacred mystery, the testimony of God to Jesus, the "record" which God gave of His Son. Let us listen in silence till the testimony is complete, until rationally impossible things, humanly absurd things, are recognized to be God's things, the truest, realest, most creative things in His new world.

Jesus Christ comes before us in the deepest strata of the New Testament tradition, as the unique "Son of God." Mark, his earliest biographer, is no mere biographer. He is a Christian witness and apologist, echoing the faith of the early Christian community in the "Gospel of Jesus Christ, the Son of God." That the Gospels grew out of this faith, namely, that Jesus Christ was the special gift of God, is indisputable, whatever be the decision of criticism regarding the particular presence in the opening verse of Mark's Gospel of the phrase "Son of God." We cannot get behind the portrait and view of Jesus presented to us by the early church. We may reject both, but we are foolish if we think that we can find a substitute for either which can claim, on grounds of objective criticism, to be truer to the original Jesus.

The churches' testimony was that God gave Jesus Christ to history in a way in which He gave no other historical figure. In Him the Word became flesh, the interpretative, creative Word of God. God incarnated Himself in Jesus for a redemptive and creative task, so that he was uniquely the Son of God. He was God manifest in the flesh, but only to the specially sensitized eye of faith which pierces behind appearances and beholds the unseen and unseeable. To any other eye, even the most sympathetic and religious eye, as it gazes upon the man of Galilee, He will appear as the greatest religious figure of history, as the one who by his precept and life revealed God most perfectly, as the absolute standard for human life, as one who undoubtedly made and had the right to make stupendous claims regarding His own importance in the coming drama of history; all of which faith, too, sees and appreciates, but it sees also that the greatest, deepest, most cosmic thing about Jesus was that "God was in Him reconciling the world unto Himself."

The word "reconciliation" brings us within sight of the cross. From the human side the cross is the culminating achievement of sin, decorously justified in the thought of its authors by the twin exigencies of the cause of God and the cause of Cæsar. Loyalty to religion and to an international civilization made the crucifixion of Jesus a logical, rational necessity. For the culture of the age, the cross was indifferent as an historical occurrence, and foolishly absurd as a religious symbol. But for a culture which owes its deepest insights and its ethical sensitiveness to Christianity, the cross presents a shattering problem. Man did it; God-believing, order-loving man, he crucified Christ. God allowed it, the God we believed to be loving, just and all-mighty. He allowed Christ to be crucified. To reflect long and deeply enough on this is to become utter skeptics, to lose faith in man and to lose faith in God.

This is one of the great insights of Dostoevsky into the meaning of the cross, when looked at solely with the eye of enlightened reason. This insight he puts into a great passage in *The Idiot*. Rogojin had been looking at a large picture of Holbein's representing the Saviour just taken from the cross.

"Lef Nicolaievitch," said Rogojin, after a pause, during which the two walked along a little further. "I have long wished to ask you, do you believe in God?"

"How strangely you speak, and how odd you look," said the other involuntarily.

"I like looking at that picture," muttered Rogojin, not noticing apparently, that the prince had not answered his question.

"That picture! That picture!" cried Muishkin, struck by a sudden idea. "Why, a man's faith might be ruined by looking at that picture."

"So it is," said Rogojin unexpectedly.

Faith in God becomes possible only if He was in that cross, and if there He was doing something to form a different kind of man from Jewish man and Roman man who between them crucified Christ, and from Grecian man who mocked at the story of the Crucified. The Christian faith is that God was in Christ. God received the NO which man hurled at Him and endured it. He suffered in Christ for human sin. There is an unfathomable meaning in the words "Jesus Christ died for our sins." To try to rationalize them and make them satisfy reason is to ask the kind of proof the Jews asked when they said that if Jesus should descend from the cross they would believe Him. Between reason and the cross there will be an unending conflict. Otherwise, the cross would cease to be the cross. But when before the cross stands not a detached spectator, but a man, broken because he has looked into the abyss of the human heart, his own and others; the words "Behold the Lamb of God who taketh away the sin of the world" sound as a gospel of hope.

Conscience, when it becomes thoroughly concerned about the question of sin, demands, as Kierkegaard has pointed out in his penetrating analysis of the human problem, the incarnation and the cross. Only a movement from God's side and on God's part, which rends the continuity of history, and breaks in an original and redemptive way into our little world, can fully satisfy one who has shamefacedly looked at his own heart and feels his need of forgiveness.

But the cross thus focused is no more than half of God's testimony to Christ. The Crucified became the Risen One. It was no message of a crucified Galilean teacher which produced early Christianity, but the message of the Crucified whom God raised from the dead. Faith in a living Lord and the experience of communion with Him introduced a spring freshness and the song of birds into a melancholic world which had lost faith in God and life. The Gospel of the Crucified-Risen One came like a thrill of dawn into human dejection. It did not come as an ethic, while bringing an ethic; it did not come as a philosophy, but it changed philosophy; it did not come as a rite, yet it produced rites; it did not come as a religion, though it became a religion. It came as faith, faith in the living One who was dead and is alive for evermore, and as a new life in Christ.

The resurrection was God's " 'yea' to man's 'nay'," as Barth puts it. What happened in the resurrection is something quite different from the mere survival of the spirit of Jesus, something much richer, much more original, much more cosmic than that. The fact of the resurrection is the concrete proclamation of God's new Kingdom in Christ, a kingdom of spiritual reality which operates in history but which is not controlled by the ordinary forces of history, a kingdom on whose frontier human society must surrender to the Lordship of God or suffer certain dissolution at the end of the road. In the resurrection, the creator God did something new, something which is the measure of the power he makes available for achievement in the human realm, something which is the pledge that for all who live by the Life, death in every phase of it shall be swallowed up in victory. Life, not death, is the real and ultimate, and the Risen Christ, as the center of God's realm, is the mediator of the life of God to men.

Two aspects of the reality of the living Christ are important elements in the complete testimony of God to Him. Between Christ and those who live by faith in Him there exists a complete interpenetration of personality. They live in Him, He lives in them.

In recent studies on Paul, Deissman and Schweitzer have both drawn attention to the fact that the central category of Paul's thought is contained in the phrase "in Christ" or "in Christ Jesus," which occurs more than one hundred and fifty times in his letters. Christians "in Christ" are at one with God and with one another. Every dividing barrier is down, both the barriers dividing God and man, and those dividing man and man. This union is something real, something which is, not something ideal, something which should be.

Herein lies the main difference between Christianity and romantic idealism. Idealism bids people follow Jesus in order to attain union with God; Christianity tells them to believe upon Christ and in Him they are already one with God. The Christian religious task consists therefore not in Christians becoming what they should be, but in becoming effectively what they really are in Christ. The social task of idealism consists in uniting people around a great ideal which transcends every individual and group interest. But no such ideal will ever be found, or become effective if it were. Human self-interest, especially the self-interest of groups, is too great to permit of deathless loyalty to ideals which have no more than a human sanction.

The primary social task of Christianity consists in a realization of the essential oneness of all true Christians in Christ, as members of that community, the church, which Paul called His Body, and in the consequent expression of that oneness across all human frontiers. In a word, let the church become as an effective international reality what it is in Christ as a spiritual cosmic reality. The form and basis of the new world order has been laid once and forever in Christ, the transcendent Christ who dwells immanently in that bruised, broken and unworthy Body, the Christian church.

"I live," said Paul, "yet not I, but Christ liveth in me." A basic element in Paul's experience of the indwelling Christ needs to be set in high relief for Christian thought and life. The Christ who was the object of Paul's preaching and the Christ who was the subject of his living was Christ Crucified, the Crucified One who had become the Risen One, the Risen One who never ceased to be the Crucified One. The living Christ of Paul, as the living Christ of the author of the Apocalypse, was a Christ for whom suffering continued to be real. The Christ whom Paul knew lived within him not as a power only, but also as a passion. It was his dearest desire to know the power of Christ's resurrection that he might know the fellowship of his sufferings. He wanted to fill up what was behind of the sufferings of Christ for His body's sake, the church.

Pascal saw deeply into this truth. "Christ," said he, "will be in agony in the souls of his people till the end of the world." In terms of this endless passion Unamuno, the

Spanish thinker, interprets Velasquez' famous painting of Christ. There is here a truth which has never been done justice either in the Catholic or the Protestant tradition. Yet it lies at the heart of Christianity.

The Risen Lord continues to agonize in a love passion in the lives of His followers. When it is realized that the sublime power of Christ's resurrection is to enable Christians to share the fellowship of His sufferings, the church will pass through an experience of rebirth, and the world will be brought nearer to believing the testimony that "God sent His Son to be the Saviour of the world."

V.

Two final questions remain. What shall be the aim of one whose personal testimony concerning Christ agrees with the New Testament testimony concerning Him, and how adequate is a message having such an origin and such content as has been indicated, to meet the modern situation?

The supreme aim of Christian evangelism must ever be to make Jesus Christ inescapable in the life of individuals and of society. This aim is not fully stated by saying that it consists in making Him known, because Christ is known, theoretically, at least, by people who take up toward Him no more than the attitude of interested spectators and kindly patrons. The world is full of Christophiles, who are not Christians, people who have made no costly or irrevocable commitment because of their knowledge of Christ.

Nor is this aim adequately formulated by saying that it consists in making Jesus Christ acceptable. Christ is taken by many people as an acceptable conclusion about life, who do not take Him as the only possible solution for life. They are interested, for one reason or another, in introducing Him into their thought categories, their cultural institutions, their religious organizations, their social programs, their political constitutions, because He helps them to think some things out and to see other things through. But they do not fit themselves and their thinking and their programs and their institutions into Him. They accept Him as a valuable servant but they will not obey Him as a sovereign Lord.

The aim of evangelism is to make Jesus Christ inescapable, the only possible solution for the human problem in its individual and social aspects. This is a task which belongs not only to preaching; it belongs equally to Christian theology, to Christian sociology and to Christian philosophy. Christ's personality and teaching, in the full testimony which they give to what God is and to what man should be, must be presented as normative for the thought and conduct of men. They constitute essentially the luminous personalization of divine law. Solely in the beam of such a light is true creative life possible. But man needs more than light and Jesus Christ is life as well as light. He is grace as well as law. As soon as the question as to the good life is raised by a person who puts the anguished question, "How shall I be able to live that kind of life, I who feel myself so unspeakably far from Christlikeness?" then Christ must be made inescapable as the answer to this question. He whose light gives rise to the question becomes Himself the answer. He who is God's ideal for life is also God's gift to life. The evangelistic task is, therefore, to make infinitely meaningful and inescapable the heart of the Gospel, God's revelation of Himself in Jesus Christ, in such a way that personality in its wholeness shall respond to God.

This message brings a word to three representative groups on the contemporary stage. It speaks to *the horizontally minded.* Horizontal-mindedness is interested only in a world of two dimensions, a world which is all surface with infinite breadth and infinite length. The horizontally minded are interested in the behavior and organization of objects human and otherwise, which move around them. They press on with ever greater celerity along a road which they call progress, which comes out of the remote past behind them and loses itself in unbroken continuity in a far horizon beyond them. Their characteristic gaze is parallel with the surface of the ground. They lack a world-view. Their representative philosophy is a philosophy of history from which certainties and ultimates are excluded. Their representative science is a study in origins and development, in terms of which they explain everything and prognosticate everything. Their representative men are executives who keep things going on the surface, the best they can in accordance with approved principles of expediency; writers and editors who keep their eyes fixed, horizontal-wise, on the eyes and every motion of their public in order to guide their literary policies; social engineers who are interested in organizing objects and human beings in such a way as to cause least obstruction and the maximum harmony on the recognized road of progress. The problem of life has become for them a problem of surface adaptation. For such a type of mind the dimension of the eternal and the absolute means nothing.

But an hour has struck in which subterranean forces have

torn great fissures in the placid surface of life, when great winds have blotted out well-trodden paths, when inhibitions of all kinds grip the souls of men and they stand still and do nothing. They are like the members of a nomad tribe after their native desert has been swept by a windstorm that obliterates the trails. No wise course is open to them but to do as the nomads do, wait for the stars to come out before continuing th. march. They are not accustomed to look up. Yet they must or perish. They need a new perspective. To a horizontally minded generation which has lost its way, our message is: Look up, sheer along the line of the vertical. Let the eternal in. We shall discover thereby the significance of life in the light of God. So shall our efforts at the organization of life on the terrestial plane, be inspired by the eternal Wisdom and undertaken through the eternal Strength.

This is a message for the *modern netherworld and its dwellers.* The break-up in actuality of the old two-dimensioned world has been followed by the apparition of an abysmal netherworld. Our generation has rediscovered hell, deep down in the human heart and in the social order. Formerly, sin was discussed academically. Now it is known practically. Its spectre stalks across the world, a world which has become converted into a great cemetery of dead values, haunted by restless, ghostly men and women whose spiritual reality has been bleached. They are in a situation and in a mood when they can begin to understand and appreciate the writings of men like Kierkegaard and Dostoevsky, who vicariously explored the netherworld of human nature, human society and human institutions. Great prayers out of the heart of the Bible are meaningful in this situation. "Make me to hear joy and gladness that the bones which

Thou hast broken may rejoice." "Oh wretched man that I am, who shall deliver me from the body of this death?"

Viewed from this angle, the contemporary situation is comparable to that tremendous vision of Ezekiel in which he saw a valley full of dry bones. The voice of God sounded in the form of a question, "Can these bones live?" This is no academic question in our time, but a terrifically practical one. God answered His own question. "Prophesy upon these bones," he said to the prophet, "and say unto them 'O ye dry bones, hear the word of the Lord.'" The divine word was echoed by human lips and lo, "there was a noise, and behold a shaking, and the bones came together, bone to his bone." When the dead lay in the form of men, covered with flesh and sinews, the divine voice again sounded: "Prophesy unto the wind, prophesy, Son of Man, and say to the wind: Thus saith the Lord God. Come from the four winds O breath and breathe upon these slain that they may live." The creative Spirit breathed and "an exceeding great army" rose from the ground.

Life is our need, life, life, life! Life that shall show Nietzsche and all neo-Nietzschians that Christianity is overwhelming abundance of life. Life that shall introduce a new meaning and thrill into our deadness, and make possible a totally new "reverence for life" such as Schweitzer pleads for, with a consequent reconstruction of life—life that shall produce Christians who literally throb and pulsate with life as did Temple Gairdner of Cairo, as does Kagawa of Japan. Such life is the gift of God. Its presence on earth will relieve us of the futility of trying to solve the human problem by the reorganization of the dead. It will make material available for the new world order we long for. The supreme need is to listen to the Word of God and to wait upon the Breath of God. Eager listening and active waiting—both in faith. The world is not resting on our shoulders. This is also a message for the *new children of our time.* One evening last June I lectured in the University of Chile. My subject was Nietzsche. Nietzsche had been the idol of more than one generation of South American youth. From him they had derived their conception of life and Christianity. A discussion of his personality and thought offered me the best possible point of contact with my audience. Interpreting Nietzsche's famous parable of the camel that became a lion and the lion that became a child, I followed modern man along the road of his measurless passion for knowledge and his iconoclastic drive toward freedom, into a fresh new childhood with wonder in its eye and a life-affirming accent on its lips. Next morning an engineering student came to see me. "I have passed through the stages you described last night," he said, in an agonized tone. "I have been a skeptic. But I cannot live on skepticism and perpetual rebellion. I need a faith. Do you think I can ever get a faith?"

An increasing number of men and women, especially of young men and women, want to give themselves to a cause, as children love to throw themselves into the arms of some one. They are looking for a master amid the confusion and dissonance of our time. They are tired of discussions, they are tired of being aimlessly free. They want to believe utterly in something, in some one; they want to be thirled to a cause worth living and dying for. They are asking for what many mentors of youth are not able to give them, for what some of these think youth should not be encouraged to seek. But youth wants to believe, it wants a supreme passion, it wants a faith. "I am dying for a faith," said a young Chinese communist girl to her judges who had condemned her to death, "What are you living for?" Never has such an opportunity presented itself to the Christian forces of the world. Either youth is helped to find in Christianity the conviction and the thrill which young nationalists and young communists find in their newfound religions, or Christianity will pass under a cloud in our time and the new crusaders will divide the world between them.

VI.

CHRISTIANITY AND OTHER WORLD RELIGIONS

IF RELIGION is at all relevant to the questions which vex the modern world, then no review of the world stiuation in which our generation finds itself can overlook the fact that hundreds of millions of human beings not only are called by the names of Mohammed or Buddha or others of the religious leaders of Asia, but look to these figures and to the religious systems associated with them for daily encouragement, solace, and uplifting.

Examination of the facts that confront us in the great countries of the East, as Africa, shows that the chaos of thought and life is even greater there than in the West. There is, as we shall see, a great drift away from religion among the educated men and women of the East. So pronounced and obtrusive is this tendency that in some circles it is considered scarcely worth while any more to devote close attention to these ancient faiths. The study is thought of as merely archæological, and irrelevant to any of the issues that really matter.

Such a judgment too easily equates the populations of the world, and the influences that moves their life, with the self-conscious and educated groups among them. Even though it is true that among the educated classes, and among the increasing population that has been drawn within the orbit of modern industrialism—a very important element—the old religions are in decay, it is not yet so with the great masses of the village population.

And even if we admit, as we ought, that the influences that possess the thinking leadership of a country must, if they are long enough continued, filter through to all strata of the people, yet it remains true that the chaos consequent upon the decay of religion as a binding force will have a character different from the chaos that is found in the West. Islam and Hinduism and Buddhism have entered far too deeply into the heart and life of the Asiatic peoples for it to be possible to ignore even the power of their decline, if decline it be.

Our plan, therefore, will be, first, to state in outline (so brief that no pretense of adequacy is suggested) what are the main teachings of the principal living non-Christian religions—for some recollection of their formal positions is necessary if modern developments are to be understood; second, to discuss some of the movements within them and the changes that are supervening upon them; and last, to consider the claim of Christianity in the light of this brief study.

Hinduism, the religion of the majority community of India, is not a "founded" religion, like Buddhism or Islam. There is no historic personality whose life and teaching are the core of the faith. It is rather the deposited religious history of the Indian race, and contains elements within itself which it would be easy to exhibit as contraries but do in fact exist together. In the early sacred books, known as the Vedas, we find a simple nature worship—the heaven, rain, fire, and the *soma* juice are among the deities. Later there came the pantheistic type of thinking about God— God was all, and was manifested in different forms.

Worked out in the philosophical books, the Upanishads, this doctrine resulted in the idea of *Brahma,* an impersonal, all-pervating essence, without attribute and beyond definition, and of the human soul, the *atman,* as one in essence with this impersonal unity of *Brahma.* There arose the system of caste, an immensely powerful social organization based partly on color, partly on religious and social function, the effect of which has been to fix the Hindu in a social group from birth, to limit his occupation, his habits, and his marriage by this group loyalty, and to support it by the most terrible religious penalties. While the highest, the Brahman or priestly, caste is removed above all others, there is below even the lower castes a mass of "untouchables," outcastes, condemned by orthodoxy to a perpetual degradation.

Three great doctrines are found among virtually all who call themselves Hindus: the Wandering or transmigration of souls; the law of *Karma,* that is, of Works, or cause and effect, whereby the lot of a soul in this life is held to be determined by its life in the previous incarnation and its behavior here to determine the next embodiment; and Release, whereby the soul, beholding Brahma and realizing its identity with Him, may get free from the chain of Wandering and Works. In the period after the rise of Buddhism there developed within Hinduism a belief in incarnations (*avatars*) of God; the most famous were two incarnations of the god Vishnu—Krishna and Rama.

The two main later developments which it is necessary

to mention are the philosophical doctrine of the Vedanta and the *bhakti* or faith-love cult of personal devotion, especially to God conceived in virtually theistic terms. The Vedanta (which is the most famous and influential of the schools of Hinduism) carries to a grimly logical conclusion the teaching of the Upanishad. Nothing truly exists but absolute Thought, Self, Brahma. He, Brahma, is "one without a second," and, in another famous text, "Thou" (human soul) "art That."

The universe of our personal life is unreal, *maya*, an illusion. Salvation lies in breaking down the illusion that keeps us from seeing that we are identical with Brahma. But the *bhakti* thinkers and poets are in revolt against this extreme monism, and they find room in the Absolute for a god whom they can worship. Moreover, they claim theirs as the true interpretation of the Upanishad. There are stories of the graciousness of God in the *bhakti* writings which show how the force of human devotion has broken through the cold rigid logic of the pantheistic system and the bleakness of *Karma*.

To all this it must be added that Hinduism is in temper not only pantheistic but also polytheistic, in that the average man worships a variety of gods, though he may vaguely admit a chief god and may hold that they are all manifestations of the one Supreme.

Buddhism, originally, was a cult or teaching that arose within Hinduism. Gautama, who came to be called the Buddha or Enlightened One, being deeply moved by the fact of suffering and having exhausted the wisdom and the austerities of the Hindu teachers of his time, attained peace in the perception of the Four Noble Truths, which are: all personal existence is bound up with suffering; all suffering is due to desire; suffering can only be removed when desire is removed; desire can only be removed by following the Noble Eightfold Path. By following this Path in its four stages the fetters of the soul are broken, including every kind of desire, even the desire for individual existence, and the devotee attains Nirvana, which may mean "nothingness" or may signify a mystical union with the ultimate.

There is underlying these truths a causal law, by which the infinite number of elements that make up the universe are ordered, and the elements of man's nature belong to this universe. But into the working of the Law desire introduces disharmony, individual life is carried on from incarnation to incarnation by the working of *Karma,* and only by the elimination of desire does the pure working of the Law move unhindered. It is an essential doctrine, therefore, that individuality is at the root of the pain of the world. But along with this metaphysic (and the monastic order in which the purity of Buddhist insight was to be perpetuated) goes a wealth of simple, racy moral teaching for the layman and the multitude, and the stories about the Buddha, his life and teaching, play a large part in ordinary Buddhist consciousness. Compassion, rooted in the character of the Buddha, is perhaps the characteristic Buddhist virtue.

The religions of China, conventionally divided as Confucianism, Taoism, and Buddhism, exhibit great differences from those of India. The central figure of Confucius is that of a practical social philosopher, and it is with the secret of strength in social and national life that the Chinese genius has wrestled, as the Indian with the nature of Reality. Confucius seems to appear in history as the representative

Chinese, and to have codified for later ages what he found in the books of the ancients. But behind him we discern three old types of religion in China, the worship of a supreme God, the worship of spirits, and the worship of ancestors.

The worship of Shang-ti, though restricted to the Emperor, did indicate the recognition of a personal supreme God beyond the medleys of current devotion. But along with that went the worship of many spirits and a way was made for idolatry. Yet the true common religion of China was the third of the types we have mentioned, the worship of ancestors, a worship immensely ancient and still living. The custom is at the basis of the strongly marked Chinese virtue of filial piety, and provides a powerful buttress to the family or clan.

Confucius' own work was to illuminate the true conditions of right living in the state and in the family. He was concerned with the typical relations of humanity—ruler and subject, father and son, elder and younger brother, husband and wife, friend and friend. Of gods and the life after death he had little to say—"We cannot yet perform our duties to men; how then can we perform our duties to spirits?" But of ethical wisdom his books are full and there is no Asiatic religious literature so free from sexual obsession.

Taoism need not detain us, for though immensely interesting as a philosophy it is found today only as superstition. Laotsze held (and so did the Confucian sages) to an original *Tao,* the way in which the universe moves, the reason of things, not Creator but perhaps Mother of all.

But Buddhism has been a great power in China and the differences between Chinese (or Northern) Buddhism and the earlier teaching, to which Ceylon and Burma more closely adhere, must be mentioned. There was added the conception of the Bodhisatvas, beings who are ready to enter upon Buddhahood but who set their bliss aside, as the Buddha himself did, for the sake of humanity. Faith in this saving Buddha becomes the most important practical feature of Buddhist religion, and still more so, as we shall see, in certain of the Buddhist sects of Japan.

In Japan it may be said that, as in China, there are three religions; the Confucian ethic, especially powerful among the educated, Buddhism, and her own indigenous Shinto, the Way of the gods. Shinto is partly nature- and spirit-worship of a primitive sort, partly an intense clan reverence. It is in this clan reverence, centered in the Mikado, originally the chieftain of a dominant tribe, that the power of Shinto is mainly expressed today. It is argued that the kind of acknowledgment of the Mikado demanded by Shinto worship is not worship but merely respect, but there are grounds for holding that the cult is virtually State-worship.

While the national expression of religious patriotism runs along Shintoist lines, it is in Buddhism that the strength of Japanese religion lies. The doctrine of the Bodhisatvas was developed in certain sects, especially in regard to the person of Amida or Amitabha. Amida is held to have appeared on earth as a monk, and gone through spiritual disciplines till he was able to return to the glorious state whence he had come. But before returning he vowed that should perfect Buddhahood be within his reach he would not accept it unless his deliverance should mean also the deliverance of mankind. In fulfilling this vow he endured much pain, but in the end he opened up a Paradise in a Pure Land, into which those may enter who have faith in him. This was the "saving vow." It is intelligible that the Jesuit missionaries on reaching Japan should have written to the Pope that they had discovered the Lutheran heresy of justification by faith! This cult is said to be the strongest religious influence within Japanese Buddhism.

Islam, the youngest of the world religions, is in its outline easy to describe, though there has been raised upon this primitive foundation a vast structure of theology and jurisprudence. "There is no god but Allah, and Mohammed is the prophet of Allah" is the call from the minarets and it is the core of the Moslem faith. Out of the idolatries of the contemporary Arab tribes—then as now not easy to unite—Mohammed forged the stark doctrine of the unity and sovereignty of Allah, and its correlative that the duty of man is submission (*Islam*) to Allah.

On this overwhelming assertion of the sovereignty of Allah all else has depended, and it is the strength of the Moslem religion. The Qu'ran is the book in which, so it is held, the words of Allah to Mohammed are set down; it is divine, it was later held to be pre-existent, and it is literally infallible and all-sufficient. Mohammed is not an incarnation, for it is supreme sin to "associate a partner with God," but he is the final prophet, the last word of God.

The institution of the Mecca pilgrimage stimulates a keen sense of the brotherhood of all Moslems (and of the corresponding low estate of all unbelievers) though there are two great divisions, the Sunnis (orthodox) and Shiahs, a minority who, in the cult of the slain grandsons of the Prophet, Husain and Husein, have some glimmerings of a notion of atonement. It should be added that there has been, at least in Moslem theory and as far as possible in

Moslem practice, an identity between church and state, the Caliph, or "successor" of the Prophet being in theory the ruler of all Moslems. The Shiahs have rejected the Caliphate idea.

There is one fact, common to all of the religions of the old world, which we may notice at this point, for it suggests the meaning of what is happening today. The great religions claimed, among other things, to provide a synthesis of the whole of life. Hinduism, for instance, was not merely a religion in the sense that it provided individual consolation; it regulated, by such institutions as caste, the whole of life. Islam has always boasted that it knew nothing of the devitalizing distinction between sacred and secular, church and state. We have omitted from our previous rapid survey any treatment of the primitive religions of Africa, but it is common ground to all students of that subject that religion and custom, the common consciousness of the tribe and the sense of individual compulsion, duty today and the fellowship of the ancestors, are all interwoven together, so that the conception of the "individual" means something foreign and incredibly difficult to the tribesman. In all these diverse modes we see expressed a common principle, namely, that the center of life, round which it is organized and in which its meaning is found, is religion.

The central truth of the condition of the world's religion today is simply this, that the ancient synthesis of life, based upon religion, has been broken into fragments. Let us look at some of the relevant facts.

A very distinguished American, known for his sympathy and love for things Chinese, said to the present writer, "Every educated man in China is either an atheist or a

Christian. Allow some measure of epigrammatic exaggeration, and the statement remains remarkable. Confucianism, despite its great prestige, is blamed for many of the evils that young China wants to sweep away—concubinage, intellectual bigotry, hypocrisy, social stagnation. In the terrific stress of the combined revolutions through which China is passing it seems that all religion, Confucianism and Buddhism alike, belongs to a bygone age, and that the only hope of the future is to reorganize life around some other center, science, perhaps, or economic ideas. Confucian scholars have urged on the Christian missions that they should lend their aid to the task of rescuing from the wreck of nihilistic revolution much that is most beautiful in the old life of China.

While all observers agree that for at least the educated classes of China religion has ceased to be a relevant issue, it is not so in Japan, for there Buddhism is a force and the national patriotism finds religious expression in Shinto. The latter, it may be, need not be taken too seriously, for it is of the essence of all Cæsarisms that a church that deifies the nation or the secular power cannot criticize it, and there is no religion, in the true sense of the word, unless there is an acknowledgment of that Sacred before which all that is in and of man has to bow. But it is significant that the sects of Buddhism, if our information may be trusted, that are most alive in Japan today are those which rest upon the Amida doctrine, in which so great a part is played by the thought of the grace of God answering the faith of the believer. For even though the "saving vow" be only a beautiful myth, it is a myth whose power points the way to truth. But while in comparison with China it may appear that there is life in Japanese Buddhism, it is also true that the rise of Communism and other "dangerous thoughts" not merely provides a problem for the administrator but points to needs and new ideas, part of the contagion of the outer world, to which Japanese religion has no reply at all to make.

It may seem absurd to say that in India, where so many religions arose, where a religious figure such as M. K. Gandhi exercises vast influence, and where it appears that the keenly religious consciousness of the Hindu and Moslem communities is a main barrier to complete self-government, there are signs, too, of a decay in religion. Yet few observers of the educated classes would deny this. For myriads of educated Indians the nationalist passion takes the place of what used to be religion; sometimes it happens that an assertion of Hindu orthodoxy is a sign of nationalist loyalty, but much more often not. One hears of the most intimate and sacred Hindu ceremonies being carried out in mocking mummery by students.

The "self-respect" movement of South India, beginning as a protest against Brahman privilege on the part of non-Brahman Hindus, went on to become a movement dedicated to two objects, the promotion of social reform and the abolition of religion. The plea is heard from the most powerful national leaders (but not from Mr. Gandhi) that there should be a separation between religion and national life; it is complained by hard-headed men that India has suffered too much by way of religious absorption.

When we look for the reasons of this movement, they are not hard to discern. On the surface, it is plain that the baser side of Indian religion repels many of the younger men and women. They loathe such institutions as child-marriage and the defences of it offered by Hindu orthodoxy. They observe the weakening of the nationalist movement by the jealousies of the great communities, and they cry, "Religion again, away with religion!"

But it is perhaps possible to go deeper. May it not be that not only by what is vilest, but by what is deepest and most real in Hinduism the keener spirits of the modern movement are repelled? There is an impatience in young India against the traditional type of holy living, an impatience with the quiescent, absorbed life of the seer, an insistence on activism, for there are things to be done in the world, abuses to be swept away, India to be freed. And on what is this quiescent mentality—what Dr. Rabindranath Tagore has called the Sudra (servant) habit based? Surely, upon that profound metaphysical doctrine to which our little sketch above made reference.

If the world is unreal, if there is a single existent Self for which attribute, quality, personality are not, if the world of moral striving is in the last analysis an unreal world, and the way of holiness is to awake out of the dream of life to know one's identity with Brahma—if this be so, then it is plain that nationalism and all the rest are just dreams, idle and empty. It was profoundly significant that at a point in Mr. Gandhi's campaign against untouchability he was severely reproved by representatives of Hindu orthodoxy on the ground that he was paying far too much attention to these mundane matters and thereby both wasting his time and doing a disservice to Hinduism.

Under such stress men will take different paths, but one thing will happen in most cases. Whether or not there is overt hostility to religion, it will cease to be the heart of life. It may still be a reality in ministering private solace; it may still add the flame of fanaticism to communal ambition; but it will become a department, not the ground of the whole. Men will find another principle by which to guide their steps; the mystery of living will be interpreted by another wisdom.[1]

Of Islam much the same tale can be told, though the intense communal pride of Islam and the simplicity of its fundamental creed delay the forces of dissolution. The unity of the Islamic church-state—never more than an ideal —is now little cherished even as ideal, for there has come into the Moslem world the force of nationalism. Turkey is far more Turkish than Moslem, and her leaders strive, by eradicating the Arabic strain from the language and by re-writing Turkish history, to minimize the place of the Islamic heritage in Turkey and to magnify the Turkish race, to which Islam is but an incident in a long career. Persia is nationalistic; Iraq is nationalistic; Copts join in Egyptian nationalism with the Moslem majority, though Egypt, fearing the example of Turkish iconoclasm, has a more definitely Moslem nationalism than elsewhere in the Near East; the Caliphate has been destroyed and with it the binding force of the common acknowledgment of the Caliph in the Friday prayers.

While the forces of secularism have been most prominent in Turkey there is overwhelming evidence to show that in Baghdad not less than Istambul, in Beirut and Tripoli, Cairo and Teheran, the classes to whom knowledge of the wider world has come, through education, literature, and travel, have ceased to believe in Islam with religious faith,

---

[1] It ought to be said that the existence of the Ramkrishna Mission, based on orthodox Hinduism, including the pantheistic philosophy and distinguished for its social service and education, is an instance, though we believe a solitary one, of orthodoxy endeavoring to meet the modern need.

whatever their position as to communal loyalty. Here again, the clash comes between the new knowledge and ideals and the rigidity of the old orthodoxy. If all truth is in the Qu'ran, then for the man of the Twentieth, not the Seventh, Century, one of two things will happen. Either he will take refuge in impossible allegorization and *tours de force* of exegesis, to make the Qu'ran say what he wants it to say, or he will abandon it if not in public, then in private.

It is a curious fact that so little, relatively, appears to have been done to fit Islam as a faith to face the needs of the modern world. It might have been expected that it would have developed into a simple Deism, offering itself as a simple faith devoid of theological complexity. In a measure it does this, but it is a notable fact that it cannot get free from the figure of Mohammed. Mohammed was obviously a figure of his time, a prophet in advance of his people and when judged by the standards of his day, as he ought to be, a very notable historical figure. But to make him a standard for humanity is frankly preposterous, and it can only be done, as we have said, by a flight of partisan exposition.

Such attempt, therefore, as is made to commend Mohammed as the Man that the world needs takes either the line of discovering in him the virtues that the world associates with Jesus, or of showing that he excels Jesus in that he is a man of the world, married, a statesman and governor, the "all-round type." Of this apologetic two things are to be said: It pre-supposes that Christians worship their Lord not as a Redeemer but as an Admirable Chrichton, and it is quite false to the Qu'ranic basis, in which Allah matters infinitely and the Prophet has not yet become the *beau idéal* of humanity.

In Africa, of which under the score of religion we have said so little, there is going on one of the great revolutions of humanity. No one can or does doubt that the tribal religions are doomed; not the missionary but the trader and administrator, the mine and plantation, have destroyed them. Where, as in Northern Rhodesia, the development of copper-mining has brought a primitive race suddenly into close touch with highly developed modern industry, we have the great modern problem of the disappearance of the religious synthesis of life in an almost classical form.

On the task of reintegrating the tribal life and helping the tribesman to become an individual much of the best brain of the world is concentrated. But no one, not even the kind of anthropologist for whom primitive humanity is a kind of game preserve, pretends that the African is going to reintegrate his life on the basis of the old worship. It is notable that in the territories of Africa under the control of the British Colonial Office it has been accepted that Christianity is to be the basis of African education.

The main fact, then, that emerges from this discussion is that an ancient synthesis is dissolving. Let it be repeated, we are not suggesting that religion has ceased to be powerful, or even that with the educated and the industrialized it has ceased to be powerful, but that it has ceased to be what supremely religion ought to be, the light in the darkness, the uniting principle, the ground to which effort and activity and ideal are referred for their validity.

Two things follow: first, that religion itself becomes a departmental thing, an interest among others, a professionalism with its own etiquette; second, that the mind and soul of man will seek until it find some other center. Of the first point it need only further be said that if the essence of secularism consists in the divorce of the parts of life from the center, so that each is a kingdom in itself—business is business, ethics and economics belong apart—then there is nothing more horribly secular in a world of secularism than religion that consents to occupy this departmental position. But of the other consideration, the rival syntheses that now arise, much might be said in another place. If Communism and Fascism are not merely political or economic doctrines but religions with the commanding power of religions, it is precisely because they claim the whole of life. Into the totalitarian state all the effort of man is gathered; the messianic dream of Communism finds in the advance of the proletariat a cause that embraces all that is in man.

What, then, of Christianity?

Two things must frankly be acknowledged. In the first place, the approach of Christianity to Africa and Asia has in the main been through members of the nations of the West which have been also in governmental and economic relation with these regions. Honesty and realism compel the confession that the color prejudice and imperialism of masses of white men constitute a barrier to the perception of the meaning of the Gospel on the part of masses of colored men. They look no further. But, in the second place, it would be insincere and partisan to write as though the Christian West had preserved a synthesis of life around the religious center while that synthesis had disappeared in the East and in Africa. All the literature of our modern world goes to deny that.

The old unified world of Europe—a world which could in a real sense be called Christendom—has gone. The infallible church has gone, the nations have arisen, deductive thinking has passed into the verifying of the hypotheses of science, the industrial revolution has created with disconcerting speed a new series of problems in social life, and it is a matter of common acknowledgment that for our age there is a chaos in place of the related sanctions of a simpler world. To urge this is not to be a mediævalist.

The changes were in God's order and the world, which is His, is the richer. But when St. Paul writes to the Colossians that all things were made in Christ and for Christ and that in Him all things hold together, he is saying something which we today can only say as an aspiration, and with the confession that we do not know what it means in the terms of our common daily life. We are divided in what we think about property, and race, and sex, and war. If we have the mind of Christ, it is a divided mind.

Yet there is more to be said than this. Whereas (and this is written without religious acrimony) it seems impossible that Mohammed of the Qu'ran, or Buddha of the passionless calm, or the Vedantist denial of the reality of moral struggle, can ever again occupy the empire of souls and minds for whom the modern world is a poignant reality, there is about the figure of Jesus an arresting quality. He is alive as these others are not. He is alive not only for His followers but for multitudes who look at Him, critically, enquiringly, wistfully, afar off.

Why is it that all these biographies of Him are written? Because there is a quality in Him from which the soul that has once seen it cannot escape. "That strange man on his cross," as Tyrrell said, "keeps calling me back." Historical criticism is a new thing in the world of Islam, and these new Mohammeds will some day have to face that withering fire, but historical criticism is native to Christian

lands, and there was never any life lived on which so searching an examination has been directed as on that of Jesus of
Nazareth. Out of it He advances toward us, one with
whom we have to make account. He is not a figure of
archæology; He is relevant to our day. More, He judges us.

This arresting quality is found not only by men of the
West but by men of the East. It is a tribute to it that the
new exposition of Mohammed is in implied defence against
the challenge of Jesus. Indians make no secret of the attraction that He has for them. It was Hindus who said to
Dr. Stanley Jones, *à propos* of Hindu-Moslem controversy,
"it is our Christian duty to love our Mohammedan brethren."

This, then, is the first great fact. Jesus Christ is alive in
the world. His attraction spreads where the witness of
Christians is feeble or without effect. But it is necessary to
go further. To take Jesus Christ seriously is to be forced
beyond a merely agnostic attitude, for He leads us into a
life in which the Father-God is the supreme reality.

Our study of the search for God, as the great religions
manifest it, shows how much men have desired to be sure
of God, and how hardly they have come to that certainty.
We have seen on the one hand the stark transcendence of
the Moslem Allah, with its consequence in the rigidity of
society, and on the other the moral defect of pantheism,
which finds God equally in everything or else eviscerates
the moral world of all meaning. We have seen, too, how
faiths in incarnation have arisen upon the human scene, and
how again and again they have failed to support the burden
of faith, for they were based on legend, and sometimes the
legend had less moral worth than the worshiper's own conscience of itself would agree to be god-like.

In Jesus Christ there is communicated to men a revelation of God as Father, a living God at work continually upon His majestic and loving purpose, one with whom man can have communion, who cares when the sparrow falls. The prophets of the Hebrews had known Him to be holy, but for the disciples of Jesus, and all men since, it has been possible to focus that holiness and love in the lineaments of a human face. As it has been said, though Jesus himself, when He wished to tell men of the love of God, uttered the parable of the Prodigal Son, when Peter and John wished to tell of that same love they spoke of the passion and death of Jesus.

The two opposites are reconciled for those who find God in Him. God is the living God, without us as our Creator and Judge, whose will it is our supreme freedom to perform, but He is also within, as He is inwardly known by the spirit that grows into the life of Christ. All this is rooted for us in history. It is not a dream, a hope, a prophet's vision. When we say that Jesus reveals God, we mean that the whole self-revelation of God to man is consummated in the historical fact of the incarnation.

This leads us to another central truth. It is a fact of deep significance that although human misery is so greatly and obviously the result of human sin, and every man of spiritual realism who looks into his own heart knows what it is that keeps him from doing the will of God, yet the great religions have so little to say about sin and so much more about suffering. There is great majesty in the doctrine of *Karma,* but it never lets us see that sin in fundamentally not just a breach in an abstract moral order, but rebellion against a living God. The Release of which the Eastern sages speak is release from the chain of mortality, the world of sense, the changes and chances of our earthly life, the haunting specter of individuality. It is not forgiveness.

We have seen, also, that in Japan and India and China there have arisen, in the Buddhist or in the Hindu tradition, stories of the gracious action of God in saving His people. No one can read these stories without being moved, for in them good men have touched the very garment of a veiled God. Yet it must be said that in these stories not only is there not the objective reality of the story of Jesus, but there is nothing of that terrible and soul-searching union of utter love—of that the East has thought much—and utter holiness.

Whatever theory of the atonement Christians accept—and none has been made *de fide* for the church—there is in the story of the cross something that not only tells of the love of God but makes it forever impossible to think easily of that love because the cost of sin to the perfect love of Christ is so plain. The Christian finds God in Christ saying to him from the cross, "Thy sins are forgiven thee; go in peace." But it is not a light thing so to be forgiven, and because it cuts so deep it brings with it release and power. To be forgiven is to find God overleaping in love the barriers man has put up by his sin; to be forgiven is to begin again as a son, doing the will of God with power, because He works in us.

A final point may be made. There is one great difference between what we may call biblical religion and all else. For the Eastern faiths this world is caught in a cycle of unmeaning recurrence; though there be infinite ages and infinite reincarnations, there is no garnered meaning in them, for they belong to the world of illusion. This is not merely an Eastern belief, for the Stoics held it too, and a

146

recent writer has suggested that one element in the victory of Christianity in the Græco-Roman world was just that it brought to men, weary of an unmeaning world, the message that there was a divine purpose being worked out, a God at work in the world, a consummation toward which the world was being led.

When the Jews think of the goodness and might of God, they think of how He brought them out of Egypt or up from exile. When St. Paul wishes to convey his sense of the omnipotence of God, he speaks of the power which He wrought in Christ when He raised Him from the dead. He is known by His mighty acts, He has visited and redeemed His people.

This deep truth surely has a bearing upon the most poignant problems of our modern world. We want to know what is the will of God in a world rapidly changing, full of new issues, and if the religion called by the name of Christ is to be for us and for the world, then we must be able to put meaning into that word of St. Paul, that "in Him all things holds together." It is, therefore, of the deepest importance that for the Christian mind God is essentially one who is at work, and that the Christian society is in the world not as the custodian of a private and mystical lore, but as the fellowship which is daily and always to be led by the Spirit in doing the will of God.

For the Christian, this world is not illusion, but neither is it the final reality. It is the school of God's teaching, the arena in which we are tested and made ready, a place where real choices are made. The reality of our world of time is the eternity that we seize within it; by the giving or the withholding of a cup of cold water we may affirm or deny the Eternal Love. So the church, with all its weaknesses and human frailty, is the fellowship of those who seek to be led by God to do His will, in this world of real action and real choice.

If a Christian may not, without deep penitence, make appeal for Christendom to the non-Christian world, he may nevertheless with joyful certainty invite all men, of all languages and kindreds, to enter together into a fellowship which is founded on nothing less than the act of God Himself. He may not ask them to desert ancient loyalties for one of his own devising, but he can witness to what God has done—that is the Gospel—and he can call them into a fellowship of love and obedience to what is greater than he or they. He cannot say "I have the solution to the problems of the world," but he can point to a Way. The church is the body of Him who said both "My Father worketh still, and I work," and also, "I have called you not servants but friends."

VII.
THE WORLD REACH OF THE CHRISTIAN FAITH

FROM its inception Christianity has been expanding geographically. Beginning as an inconspicuous Jewish sect, one of the least of the many cults seeking to make a place for themselves in the Græco-Roman world, it early outgrew its Jewish swaddling clothes, became cosmopolitan in membership, and within less than four centuries was the dominant faith of the Roman Empire. When the Roman Empire collapsed, Christianity, although by that time closely associated with it, not only survived but won to its fold the barbarians who were the immediate cause of the overthrow, spread into regions in Northern and Western Europe which had not before known it, and became the chief vehicle for the transfer of the culture of the ancient world to the Europe of mediæval and modern times. In the middle ages Christianity was an integral part of the intellectual, social, economic, and political patterns of the day. Its theology was formulated in terms of the prevailing scholasticism and it was apparently a bulwark of the existing feudal society.

Yet when the mediæval world disappeared, Christianity persisted. Not only so, but when, in the Fifteenth and Sixteenth Centuries, European peoples spread into the Americas and won footholds in Asia, Christianity went with them, became the faith of the peoples whom the Europeans conquered, and ameliorated the cruelties of the conquest. When, in the Nineteenth and Twentieth Centuries, European peoples again expanded, colonizing fresh sections in the Americas, occupying all of Africa and the islands of the Pacific, and subjecting to their control much of Asia, Christian missions followed and in some instances anticipated the advancing frontiers of Occidental power, and modified profoundly the revolutionary results of the impact of Western upon non-Western peoples and cultures.

Occasionally Christianity has suffered major territorial reverses. In the Seventh and Eighth Centuries Islam won from it vast areas and numerous peoples. In the Fourteenth and Fifteenth Centuries the wide-flung posts of Nestorian Christianity in Asia were almost wiped out by Tamerlane and his cohorts. In the present century the church in Russia has been dealt staggering blows. Yet in spite of the fact that Christianity has never fully regained the ground from which it was driven in these defeats, usually it has more than made good in other regions the area lost. Never has it been so widespread as today.

In the history of mankind no other religion has been professed over so large a proportion of the globe or by so many people. From the outset Christianity has claimed for its message universality: it has maintained that it has a gospel for all men. More nearly than any other faith it has progressed toward the attainment of that goal. While of the other two great surviving missionary religions, one, Buddhism, has long been practically stationary, and the other, Islam, has made few if any major gains in the past hundred years, Christianity, in spite of the many obstacles which beset its path, is still spreading. In no similar length of time have its boundaries expanded so rapidly and so widely as in the past century and a half.

During the nearly two thousand years of its existence, and in the course of its spread, Christianity has inevitably been modified by its environment. In many respects the Christianity of the Fourth Century, when the Roman Empire made peace with and espoused it, differed markedly from that of the First. The Roman Catholic Church of the middle ages—then the Church of Western Europe—displayed contrasts with the Church of the Byzantine Empire. The Protestantism of Germany is readily distinguished from that of Great Britain, and American Protestant Christianity is not identical with either. Christianity, indeed, has presented and still presents a multitude of aspects and forms. It has in part taken on the color of each class, nation, and people which has adopted it, and has been modified by every age through which it has lived. Yet all its many forms have striking family likenesses. The faith enunciated and lived by Jesus and his immediate disciples has had a strange vitality and something of its lineaments can be observed even in the Christian bodies which have departed most widely from the original.

Moreover, wherever Christianity has been adopted by any considerable number of people, it has had an effect, usually very profound, upon its environment. It is, to be sure, often difficult if not impossible to determine how far a given movement is the product of Christianity and how far the result of other factors. It is clear, for example, that modern international law owes its inception in part to a Spanish churchman and was given its classic formulation by a devout Dutch Protestant, Hugo Grotius. Yet some of the basic ideas to which these writers appealed are clearly not of

Christian origin, and it is practically impossible to ascertain whether international law as we now know it would have come into existence without the Christian impulse.

So, too, it is clear that Christianity has had an enormous part in the transformation of the Scandinavians from the roistering pirates who, a thousand years ago, terrorized much of Western Europe, into the highly civilized peoples of today. On the other hand, it is also obvious that Christianity has not been the sole cause of the change. However, even on many movements which cannot be said to be exclusively or even predominantly its product, the stamp of Christianity is evident, and of some it can be said that they would not be in existence but for the Christian message. Thus the end of the international slave trade and of slavery within the British Empire were clearly the work of Wilberforce and those associated with him, who owed their reforming zeal to the impulse they derived from the Evangelical Awakening. Who of us, too, has not known individuals completely transformed morally and spiritually by contact with the Christian Gospel?

What the average intelligent Protestant Christian of today more or less vaguely has in mind when he hears the word "missions" is but one portion of this nearly two thousand-year-old and world-wide expansion of Christianity. It is, however, an extremely important segment of it. By it is meant the spread in the past hundred and fifty years of Protestant Christianity, through societies and the agents appointed by them, into Asia, Africa, the islands of the Pacific, and Latin America—areas which might be called "the new frontiers of the churches." This "modern missionary movement" is usually thought of as having its beginning in William Carey, who, in 1792, brought about the formation of the (British) Baptist Missionary Society and himself later gave many years of distinguished service in laying the foundations for Protestant Christianity in India.

It was foreshadowed by the remarkable Moravian missions which, emanating from Herrnhut, had their beginning in 1732, and by still other and even earlier developments. The formation of the (British) Baptist Missionary Society was followed in the next three decades by the organization of other societies in Great Britain, Europe, and America, some of them the strongest of the present time. In the United States the oldest are the American Board of Commissioners for Foreign Missions (1810) and the predecessor of the American Baptist Foreign Missionary Society (1814) both of which arose out of the efforts of a group of students led by Samuel J. Mills and Adoniram Judson.

This modern Protestant missionary movement has been predominantly, although by no means exclusively, Anglo-Saxon. By far the major part of its personnel and financial support has been drawn from Great Britain, the United States, Canada, Australia, and New Zealand. Its religious impulse has come primarily from the Evangelical Awakening of the Eighteenth Century and the movements which historically have been rooted in that revival.

The new tides of Christian faith and life associated with such names as Jonathan Edwards, John Wesley, and Whitefield and continuing in the revivals of the Nineteenth Century and in the work of such individuals as Dwight L. Moody, overflowed from the British Isles and the United States, had their effects throughout much of Protestantism, and helped to give rise to societies for the propagation of the Christian Gospel the world over. The aspirations to which they gave birth expressed themselves in the courageous and challenging watchword "the evangelization of the world in this generation," which so stirred student Christian circles of the closing decades of the Nineteenth and the opening decade of the Twentieth Century.

This Evangelical Awakening and the revivals which succeeded it had as their primary objective the regeneration of individuals—the creation of transformed and ennobled personalities. It was based upon a conviction of the infinite worth of every human soul, no matter how degraded it might seem to be, and upon the power of God to remake all who give themselves in faith to Him. Closely and in Anglo-Saxon lands almost inseparably associated with this objective were movements for the eradication of collective ills and the improvement of the social environment.

Prison reform, the abolition of Negro slavery, the temperance movement, better educational opportunities for the masses, and the struggle to eliminate war were only some of the more striking of the crusades for human betterment which either had their origin in the religious awakening or were greatly re-enforced by it. Both of these major objectives of the revived Protestantism have characterized Protestant missions.

Moreover, the Protestant missionary movement has been part and parcel of the remarkable expansion of European peoples and culture which has been so outstanding a feature of the history of the world in the Nineteenth and Twentieth Centuries. In the course of the past hundred and fifty years every portion of the globe has felt the impact of the West. Under the force of that impact, the majority of non-Occidental civilizations have either collapsed or been profoundly modified.

Thus the old tribal organizations of Negro Africa and their attendant customs are disappearing; nationalist Turkey is deliberately abandoning many of the distinctive features of the past and is assuming European garb; the Indian Nationalist Congress, seeking to throw off what it deems the British political and economic yoke, assembles by means of railways and automobiles and carries on its deliberations in English; all of China's institutions are in a state of flux; and Japan has maintained its political independence and become one of the major powers by sacrificing its isolation and Occidentalizing its life. It is sometimes said that a world culture is in process of emerging, but, if that is the case, thus far its features are of Western provenance.

The primary motive which has led European peoples thus to penetrate and subjugate the world has been economic. With the arrival of the machine age and with the increased production which has accompanied it, the world has been ransacked for raw materials for factories, fresh sources of labor have been developed among native peoples of Africa, Asia, and the Pacific for the plantations and the mines from which some of these raw materials are derived, and every possible market has been exploited. "Imperialism," the subjugation of enormous areas, has followed. Political and economic penetration has unavoidably been accompanied and followed by revolutionary cultural changes.

Side by side with the economic and political expansion of the West have gone Christian missionaries. Sometimes, as in the case of David Livingstone, they have been in the advance, at others they have been contemporaneous, and in some places they have lagged behind. Occasionally missionaries have had an important part in obtaining the extension of the control of their government over the area in which they have labored, and so have been agents of Western imperialism. Much more frequently they have had little or no part in encouraging political conquest.

However, to see in missions simply a phase of the exploitation of non-European peoples by the West is so to distort the facts as to make them quite out of accord with reality. To view them in their true perspective, one must regard them as the effort of earnestly Christian folk, usually a small minority of European and American peoples, to make the impact of the West upon non-Occidental races a blessing and not a curse. Where the trader saw in the geographic discoveries of the Eighteenth and Nineteenth Centuries an opportunity for commerce and for financial profits for himself, the missionary and those who have supported him have seen a challenge to bring the "Glad Tidings" to all men. When they have sung, as have thousands of supporters of missions for more than two centuries,

> "Blessings abound where'er he reigns;
> The prisoner leaps to lose his chains;
> The weary find eternal rest,
> And all the sons of want are blessed"

they have voiced their faith in what they have believed the message of Christ could do for the world.

In its outpouring of life and treasure, in the main unselfish, the Christian foreign missions of the past hundred and fifty years are unequalled in magnitude by any other religious movement in the history of the human race. The two largest divisions of the Christian Church, Roman Catholicism and Protestantism, have actively participated in it. Tens of thousands of men and women have given their lives as missionaries. They have gone to the icy wastes of the Arctics and to the enervating heat and the disease-infected jungles of the Tropics. They have braved ill-health, persecution, misunderstanding, and separation from their families, and have undertaken the difficult task of mastering alien languages and adapting themselves to unaccustomed and often uncomfortable methods of living with no thought of personal gain.

Their work has been made possible by the gifts, aggregating, in the course of a century and a half, hundreds of millions of dollars, contributed by millions of Christians. Many of the contributors have given sacrificially, out of their poverty, and few of the donors have had any personal contact with those who they have believed would be benefited by their gifts. They have contributed of their substance in behalf of peoples whom most of them would never see and of whom they knew but little. Never, not even in the first Christian centuries, has there been such lavish support of missions to distant lands by the rank and file of Christians.

In the Roman Empire Christianity spread largely by personal contacts and not through professional missionaries. In the Middle Ages and in the Sixteenth and Seventeenth Centuries there were missionaries, but they were financed chiefly by the state. In the Nineteenth and Twentieth Centuries, while some assistance has been afforded by governments, usually in the form of subventions to schools, the bulk of the expense has been met by the voluntary contributions of thousands of private individuals. Moreover, no single century in human history has ever seen so many missionaries go forth in behalf of any faith as have the past ten decades in the modern Christian missionary enterprise. It has been and is a most amazing movement.

The methods by which Protestant missionaries have carried on their work have been multiform. Nor has there been complete agreement as to objectives and procedures. Protestant missions have been conducted by boards and societies, several score in number. Though many are undenominational, most of them draw their support from specific communions. All, including the nominally undenominational ones, tend to represent particular points of view and to differ in their ideals and programs. Moreover, even the individual missions supported by a particular board may adopt different methods. This variety of ways in which missionaries approach their task has its weaknesses, but it makes for freedom in experimentation and for richness of contribution to the peoples among whom they work.

Amid all this diversity, however, has been a surprising amount of uniformity. Protestant missionary methods have tended to develop in certain main directions. One of these is what is usually designated evangelism—presenting in an intelligible fashion a knowledge of the Christian faith and winning the hearer to acceptance. This is often thought of as the primary purpose of missions. Closely allied with it is the assisting to birth and independent life of some form of Christian community. Repeatedly the objective of missions is declared to be the creation of self-supporting, self-governing, self-propagating churches. Most missionaries have believed their task incomplete if they contented themselves with spreading abroad the Christian message and leading people to enter the Christian life. They have conceived it to be their function as well to assist these new-born Christians into further stages of a Christian experience and to group themselves into congregations which will in time, quite independently of the foreigner and his financial assistance, be vital units of the world-wide Church of Christ.

A third method, also nearly related to the first two, is the creation of a Christian literature in the vernacular. This has often involved, as a necessary preliminary, the reduction of a language to writing. It has also included the translation of part or all of the Bible, of catechisms or some other summary of Christian teaching, of hymns, of service books, and, in some of the major languages, the publishing of periodicals and the writing of books and pamphlets.

A fourth method, also, at least in its inception, akin to these others, has been education. The church and the school have gone hand in hand. Protestantism has had as one of its tenets the privilege of each Christian to read the Bible for himself, and, accordingly, a literate church has generally been a missionary objective. Because in most lands to which missionaries go the percentage of illiteracy is very high, this has often necessitated the creation of a system of primary schools. Moreover, teachers for these schools and pastors for the rising churches have been needed, and to train them secondary and higher schools have been added. Since in many lands non-Christians as well as Christians have been eager for education of a Western type, and the missionary has often been the only one at hand to give it, mission schools have frequently taught more non-Christians than Christians. Missionaries have been willing to enroll non-Christians in their schools, partly because they have seen in this an opportunity to introduce students to the Christian life and to build Christian character, and partly because they have heard here a call to help meet a felt need for a type of education better adapted than the old to the new age into which the lands of their adoption are being hurried by the impact of the West.

A fifth missionary method has been that of medicine. Western medical science is so vast an improvement over the methods of treating disease in vogue in most of the lands in which missionaries reside that they have believed it their duty, as followers of the Great Physician, to employ it to relieve the suffering about them. In medicine, too, they have seen a means of winning a sympathetic hearing for the spoken and the printed message which they have come to bring.

Medicine is by no means the only way in which missionaries have sought to meet physical and moral distress. They have often initiated or joined in famine relief. As a means of preventing famine and mitigating poverty they have introduced improved methods of agriculture. They have begun cooperative rural banks, they have built model houses in industrial centers, they have organized public health programs, they have brought in athletic sports and organized better recreation. They have fought slavery, opium, the liquor traffic, and prostitution. They have been responsible for organizations for bettering international relations.

In all of these tasks missionaries and mission boards have become aware of a need for cooperation. As a result, nowhere in the Protestant world has such advance toward joint planning and action been achieved as in the foreign missionary enterprise. In each of the lands from which missionaries are sent most of the boards join in a body for united counsel—in the United States and Canada the Foreign Missions Conference of North America. In most of the lands or areas to which missionaries go are what are usually called National Christian Councils. All these, in turn, appoint representatives to The International Missionary Council, in which more of Protestantism effectively cooperates than in any other one organization.

The missionary thinks of his task—at least in its present form—as temporary. He has, accordingly, sought to recruit and train natives of the land to which he has gone to take over the leadership and financial maintenance of the institutions which he has called into existence and so to make himself unnecessary.

Inevitably the question emerges of the results which have followed the missionaries and their methods. It is difficult accurately to determine and appraise these, for many of the most vital are in the realm of the intangible which defy measurement and often even elude detection. Here, too, each observer's bias must be reckoned with. However, some results seem fairly clear.

First, and in some ways most important of all, the missions of the past century and a half have led to the emergence of Christian communities in each of the lands in which they have been conducted. In some places, notably in several of the islands of the Pacific, the majority of the population has become at least nominally Christian. In no large country, however, are the new Christian communities more than a small minority of the population. Including Roman Catholics, in Japan and China it is less than one per cent, in India about one and one-half per cent, in Negro Africa between two and three per cent, and in Persia and the Near East, except for those groups which have come out of the fellowship of the older Oriental churches, numerically almost negligible. In Latin America the groups which have arisen out of Protestant missions are also only a very small percentage of the total population.

Yet in practically all of these lands the percentage of increase has been and is much more rapid than that of the population as a whole. While at the rate of growth which has prevailed in the past hundred and fifty years the time is far distant when professing Christians will number a majority among the peoples of any land, in most countries each decade sees them constituting a larger proportion of the whole. In a number of regions, moreover, as in Uganda, among the Karens in Burma, and among the colored and black peoples of the Cape Province of the Union of South Africa, those calling themselves Christians are either in a clear majority or constitute a very substantial minority of the groups of which they are a part.

The nature of these Christian churches varies from country to country. Thus in Japan Protestants tend to be drawn from the upper middle urban class; in China they come from a large number of different groups and from both city and country; in India those of a low caste or outcaste background largely predominate; and in the Near East, as has been suggested, most of them are not from Islam but from the older Christian churches.

In practically every land the Protestant Christian groups are growing not only in numbers but in vitality. In many places or viewed simply at any one time, there often seems to be a discouragingly parasitic dependence of the local congregations on foreign money and a disheartening dearth of indigenous leadership. However, taking any large country as a whole, and especially when one looks over the younger churches the world around, the last decades have seen notable progress in financial self-support, earnestness in spreading the faith, and leadership.

One must ask, too, what membership in the church has

meant to the individual Christian. Many have entered the church from a mixture of motives, in some instances with the hope of improving their economic status or obtaining an education. Second and third generation Christians who have been reared in the church are often partly deracinated and Westernized, and (much like similar Christians in Europe and America) take their faith for granted. However, for many conversion means satisfaction of a spiritual hunger, freedom from the chains of degrading habits, and moral regeneration. Both the new converts and those nurtured in the Christian faith tend to approximate more closely to the Christian virtues than do the non-Christian stocks from which they are sprung, and in lands where illiteracy is high and sanitation low, to be much above the average in literacy and cleanliness.

Moreover, it must be noted that among their respective peoples Christians have a much larger influence proportionately than their numbers would lead the observer to expect. Thus in Japan the Protestant community, which is only about one-tenth of one per cent of the nation, has produced many leaders in education, in politics and in social reform (notably, at the present time, Kagawa). In China, Sun Yet-sen, who more than any other Chinese of the present century has molded his country and has tended to bring high-minded idealism into the selfish welter of Chinese politics, received his formal education at the hands of Protestant missionaries and was a professing Christian; a large proportion of the leaders who in building the new national government are bringing order out of chaos are baptized Protestant Christians; and some of the most notable molders of the new education are of that faith. The two best known and most influential Indians of our day, Mahatma Gandhi and Rabindranath Tagore, while not calling themselves Christian, are very different men because of Christian factors which have entered into their development.

Missionaries have promoted friendly international understanding. In some instances they have made for friction and more than once they have presented to their supporting constituencies the vices rather than the virtues of the peoples among whom they have labored. However, from among Protestant missionaries have come some of the most notable sympathetic and well-informed interpreters of the peoples of Asia to the English-speaking world, and such an organization as the Institute of Pacific Relations is a direct product of the missionary enterprise.

In education, missionaries have led in helping in the transition from the older to the modern types of schools. While, with the development of government institutions, in some countries that leadership has passed or is passing, in many others missions still maintain practically the only schools available.

In China missionaries have led in the formation of a modern medical profession, and in numbers of other lands their physicians and hospitals have had and have a notable part in healing disease.

In many another form of ameliorating social conditions missionaries have been pioneers—in famine relief, in care for the orphaned, the blind, the lepers, and the insane, in improved agricultural methods, in sanitation, in better housing conditions, and in the fight against slavery and opium. The status of Christian women is a vast advance, in education, in freedom, and in self-respect, over their non-Christian sisters about them. In the Orient the woman's movement owes an incalculable debt to the missionary.

All this may seem to be in the nature of a biased argument for missions. It is not meant to be such. It is, however, written out of a profound conviction that a dispassionate survey of the course of the spread of Christianity shows the Gospel to have been a source of movements which have made for the betterment of mankind, and that this has never been more the case than on those fresh geographic frontiers of Christianity where the foreign missionary enterprise of the past hundred and fifty years has been at work. With all of its faults, and they are many, the modern missionary movement has been an outpouring of the life of the churches of Europe and America which is counting on the side of making the pressure of the West on non-Western peoples a blessing and not an unmitigated curse.

VIII.

THE PURPOSE OF MISSIONS

THE Christian mission, writes Professor Hocking, "is based on a religious certainty and imperative—not first of all on a humane disposition toward distant lands." The missionary motive is the twofold motive of the Christian life—love to God and love to fellowmen. It is the natural, valid human impulse to share the deepest insights, the supreme values, the basic truth in which one finds the secret of life.

This conception of the missionary motive was clearly stated in the Message of the Jerusalem Meeting of the International Missionary Council: "Our true and compelling motive lies in the very nature of the God to whom we have given our hearts. Since He is love, His very nature is to share. Christ is the expression in time of the eternal self-giving of the Father. Coming into fellowship with Christ we find in ourselves an overmastering impulse to share Him with others. . . . He Himself said, 'I came that they may have life, and may have it abundantly,' and our experience corroborates it. He has become life to us. We would share that life."

This does not mean that the particular forms in which Christian truth has been formulated or Christian institutions organized are sacrosanct, to be transmitted without change to those with whom we would share Christ. The Council was keenly awake to possible and actual misconceptions and abuses of the missionary motive, and undertook decisively and explicitly to eliminate these. To share Christ is to share freedom. "The Gospel by its very nature and by its declaration of the sacredness of human personality stands against all exploitation of man by man. . . . We cannot tolerate any desire, conscious or unconscious, to use this movement for purposes of fastening a bondage, economic, political, or social, on any people. . . . We repudiate any symptoms of a religious imperialism that would desire to impose beliefs and practices on others in order to manage their souls in their supposed interests. We obey a God who respects our wills and we desire to respect those of others. . . . Nor have we the desire to bind up our Gospel with fixed ecclesiastical forms which derive their meaning from the experience of the Western church. Rather the aim should be to place at the disposal of the younger churches of all lands our collective and historical experience. We believe that much of that heritage has come out of reality and will be worth sharing. But we ardently desire that the younger churches should express the Gospel through their own genius and through forms suitable to their racial heritage. There must be no desire to lord it over the personal or collective faith of others."

Here and elsewhere in the proceedings of the Council, it is stated or implied that sharing is not imposition; neither is it one-sided, but a fellowship wherein both parties give and both receive. It is implied, moreover, that Christianity as we at present understand and practice it is not final and complete, seamless and without flaw. There is truth in Christ yet to be learned, power still to be gained. We are not as those who have fully attained and are perfect. The experience of sharing puts our religion to the test. It reveals what is gold and what is wood, hay, or stubble. It helps us to discover what is strong and what is weak, what is essential, vital and permanent, and what is relatively external, mechanical and transient, in that complex of divine and human elements which constitutes present-day Christianity.

Let us distinguish five aspects of Christianity, which for convenience may be termed its dimensions:

(1) Christian ethics

(2) The Christian gospel

(3) Christian discipleship

(4) Christian creeds

(5) Christian polities

(1) *Christian ethics.* Christianity is a way of life—a way of living and a way of judging life's values. We may admit that we do not see all of the implications of Jesus' teaching concerning life and conduct; and we must in all honesty confess that our own practice falls short of the ideals which we profess. We may grant, too, that Jesus lived under simpler conditions, and that we can not expect him to furnish detailed legislation, rules, road-maps, or blue-prints for the more complex life of our time. Yet the principles of the good life which he taught by precept, parable, and example are foundational, permanent, and true.

Jesus Christ asserted the supreme worth of persons, and regarded things as of secondary, instrumental value. He expounded the Golden Rule as a matter of downright, elemental fairness. He affirmed that ethical love—good will based upon respect for personality—is the central principle and motive of good living. He taught men to estimate all goods and all greatness in terms of human service. He emphasized the dependence of overt action upon that which is within, upon the issues of heart and imagination, the secret springs of thought and motive. He demanded the stripping away of all sham, pretence, and insincerity, and encouraged men to live true, straightforward, honest and fearless lives. He saw that love always means self-discipline and self-denial, and that the seeds of achievement are sown in sacrifice.

The Christian seeks to apply these ethical principles, not only in his immediate contacts and associations with other individuals, but to the whole body of human relations and institutions. Christ's conception of the Kingdom of God was a vision of a new social order, issuing from a new relation of individual men to the Father of their being. In our time, the Christian is here confronted with problems of peculiar urgency and unprecedented difficulty, the solution of which demands of him not only sincerity but intelligence, openness of mind, and willingness to learn, as well as courage and the spirit of adventure.

The principles themselves are clear-cut. There is no haziness in Jesus' ethical teaching. The great difficulty lies in the fact that we live up to it so poorly. As individuals, measured upon this dimension, most of us are but part-Christian. As societies and nations, we are more than half pagan. Yet whatever of strength, stability, and lasting worth our present life contains, is manifestly at those points where we are nearest to basing it upon Jesus' principles.

(2) *The Christian gospel.* The Christian gospel is Jesus'

revelation of the character and disposition of God. Jesus' way of life was grounded in His understanding of the nature of Reality. Love, forgiveness, mercy, sincerity, and good will are principles of His ethical teaching, not because they are ideal aspirations of his own, or because men have agreed to regard these as virtues, but because they lie at the heart of the universe. God has these qualities. God is love, forgiveness, mercy, grace, and truth.

Jesus accepted the conception of God which the great Hebrew prophets had proclaimed. He took for granted the high and pure ethical monotheism, the conceptions of the goodness and justice of God, and the truths concerning the creative and sustaining relation of God to the universe which had been revealed to men through them. He did not undertake by argument to prove God's existence and character, nor even to discuss His attributes in any complete way, so far as our records show. All this He assumed. It was part of the Hebrew heritage. He came not to destroy, but to fulfil the law and the prophets.

But Jesus went beyond the Hebrew prophets, and set himself in marked opposition to the current legalism and apocalypticism which were the decadent successors of prophecy, in his teaching of the Fatherhood of God. Without any loss of the principle of God's sovereignty, and without any blurring over of His justice, Jesus' characteristic and constant emphasis is upon the character and disposition of God as the Father of men. He revealed God as loving men, caring for individuals as well as for nations, seeking men to be His children, hearing and answering their prayers as a parent would his child's request, forgiving freely their folly and wrong, redeeming them from sin, and empowering them to newness of life.

Let it be granted, as it must be, that the being of God lies beyond the power of our finite minds fully to comprehend and formulate; let it be granted that all human analogies are but symbols of His infinite, exhaustless Reality; yet we follow Christ in affirming that the least inadequate symbols, the forms of thought and speech that most nearly approximate what we know and may believe about God, are drawn from the relations that ideally hold between parent and child. God is no mere king, or judge, or exacting creditor; He is a Father, loving, gracious, merciful, and infinitely patient. The Kingdom of God is not arbitrary, vindictive, cataclysmic. The Kingdom of God is "the reign of divine love exercised by God in His grace over human hearts believing in His love and constrained thereby to yield Him grateful affection and devoted service." [1] This is the gospel—the good news—that Christ came to bring.

(3) *Christian discipleship.* Christ not only *taught* this gospel—this good news—about the character and disposition of God. He himself *was* the gospel. He lived it. In him the character and disposition of God "dwelt among us, full of grace and truth." If we try, by the farthest stretch of imagination, to conceive what God would be like were He to assume flesh and be as one among men, we cannot get away from the character and disposition of Jesus Christ. He would be like Jesus. Discussions concerning the divinity of Christ too often proceed upon a logical basis quite contrary to fact. The question is asked, Was Jesus divine? as though we first knew what God is like and could then

---

[1] That belief in God's sovereignty and trust in His Fatherhood are not incompatible, as some would today have us believe, is evidenced by the fact that this statement is quoted from Professor A. B. Bruce, the eminent Scotch theologian, of strict Calvinistic heritage, and a staunch upholder of the principle of divine sovereignty.

undertake to compare Jesus with Him. The fact is just the opposite. It is Christ whom we know, and our question must be: Is God like Christ? Is God what Christ revealed Him to be?

To that question the Christian answers Yes. However far above and beyond our limited minds the being of God may lie, however rightly reverence shrinks from the attempt to encompass Him in fragile concepts and partial definitions, it is the faith of the Christian that in Christ we stand face to face with ultimate Reality, we catch a vision of the heart and will of God. It is not merely as an ethical teacher, nor even as an example of what human life may be, that Jesus Christ is the central figure in human history. It is because He affords us a glimpse of the ultimate Power, the final Law, the supreme Will, with which we have to do; because we see in him the character and disposition of God living among men.

That vision is redemptive; it has power to lift men out of meanness and pettiness and sin, out of bondage by lust and fettering by habit. It makes possible the fellowship with God in prayer and in action which recreates desire, awakens insight, and assures self-control. It brings salvation, not just beyond death, but here and now. God is in Christ, reconciling the world unto Himself. And when we affirm belief in the living, eternal Christ, we declare our conviction that the character and disposition of God thus revealed is consistently true and forever dependable.

The Christian is a disciple of Jesus Christ. He believes Christ, believes in him, trusts him, and is loyal to him. Such trust is more than intellectual assent to propositions about Christ, more than verbal professions of faith in him. It is intensely practical, a basing of life and action upon the relation to God into which we have entered through Christ. "Not every one that saith unto me, Lord, Lord, shall enter into the Kingdom of Heaven; but he that doeth the will of my Father who is in heaven."

In the early centuries of the Christian church the candidates for baptism, renouncing Satan and all his works and ways, made covenant with Christ in a striking phrase: "I enlist with thee, O Christ." That is a literal translation of the Greek words of the covenant. It is a military term that was used. It pledged one to the loyalty of a soldier. The man who took that vow of allegiance thereby acknowledged Christ as the Captain of his salvation and Lord of his life, and enlisted for service under him. It might be well if more of that objective, militant spirit possessed us; if we realized more fully that Christian discipleship is enlistment for service, and that the fight against lust and greed and wrong, within us and about us, constitutes an ample and robust "moral equivalent of war."

(4) *Christian creeds.* As we pass to the Christian creeds, we are on less sure ground. Let us include in this dimension all doctrines and dogmas that go beyond the revelation of the character of God in Jesus Christ.

The doctrinal development of Christianity has been inevitable and necessary, for intellectual reasons. It has resulted from reflection on the meaning and import of the Christian gospel and on the relation of Christ himself to the gospel; from the interpretation of expanding and deepening Christian experience; and from attempts to state the Christian convictions in terms generally intelligible because consonant with current concepts and language. Christians cannot avoid thinking; they should not avoid thinking. They ought rather to cultivate it. And it is inevitable that they should think, not only of how to apply in practice the principles of Christian ethics and the Christian gospel, but also of the setting in theory of these principles themselves. So doctrines have been elaborated concerning such problems as the metaphysical relation of Christ to God, the union of the divine and human in Christ, the relations of the persons in the Trinity, the nature and processes of divine inspiration, the manner and date of the second coming of Christ, the nature of the resurrection and the conditions of life beyond death.

Some of the doctrines so emerging are of tremendous importance; others more or less unessential. Some are clearly justified inferences from the primary data and true interpretations of Christian experience; others are more dubious. Some have been enacted into dogma, or find place in the historic confessions of the Protestant churches; others remain unstamped by any such authority. These differences bear evidence, not to the weakness or inadvisedness of the total doctrinal development of Christianity, as is sometimes assumed, but rather to its richness and vitality. I find myself in hearty agreement with what Professor Hocking wrote some years ago, *à propos* of Mr. Wells' insistence that the Christian creeds must be revised and simplified:

"I doubt whether the revision now needed is what has commonly been meant by that term—a trimming off of superfluities, a weeding out of errors, a search for a final formula for the 'essence' of the faith—all in the interest of maximal agreement upon a minimal platform. There is no virtue in a minimum of faith. For three centuries it has been the creed of the attacker of creeds that believers have believed too much. We must repudiate this stupid program of self-impoverishment. For religious experience, like that of science or art, is cumulative, and mankind normally grows richer with time, not poorer. The revision now needed is rather in the interest of making as much as possible as intelligible as possible."

It should be added that when we succeed in making as much as possible as intelligible as possible, we shall see more clearly the differences between those doctrines which are intrinsic and essential interpretations of the Christian gospel and other doctrines which, however legitimate and even true, are not thus intrinsic and essential, and yet other doctrines for which the evidence is so little decisive that they remain proper ground for the exercise of the individual believer's judgment and choice.

(5) *Christian polities.* By the Christian polities let us understand, not only systems of church government, but the whole body of the practices of the Christian churches, embracing cult and discipline as well. No intelligent Christian tries to live to himself or to fulfil his discipleship alone. He finds fellowship in a community of Christians; he joins a Christian church. Joining a church, he finds rites, customs, rules, and a plan of organization, which become henceforth a part of his heritage. He may reject certain parts of that heritage, he may modify it in such fashion that it will be quite changed for all who come after him—as Luther, Knox, and Calvin did—yet the heritage is there. Churches cannot exist without some such body of laws, customs, and institutions.

It is with respect to this dimension that the Christian churches differ most. If we can imagine a visitor from some other planet converted by an angel to Christian discipleship, and under the tutelage of his heavenly mentor understanding and accepting the Christian ethics, the Christian gospel, and even the more fundamental doctrines of the Christian creeds, and then set down in an American city, there to live and fulfil his discipleship to Christ, we can also imagine his astonishment when he contemplates joining a church. Having been converted by an angel, and being set down in a strange land, he has no such ties to determine his choice as settle that matter for most of us.

It is a serious decision for him to make. He realizes that he cannot serve Christ effectively alone; and he wishes to unite himself to the church which is unmistakably and wholeheartedly the true church of Christ. So he asks the angel which church he should join; but the angel is on this point strictly neutral, and replies that he must choose for himself.

"What are the differences?" he wants to know.

"They are of many kinds," the angel answers. "You may be governed by bishops or by synods or by conferences or by nothing except the vote of your own local group. You may be served by a minister ordained by the people who called him to be their leader in spiritual things, or by a priest ordained by the laying on his head of the hands of a bishop who had been ordained by the laying on his head of the hands of a bishop who had in his time been so ordained by one who had been so ordained by someone else, and so on back in unbroken succession to the Apostle Peter. You may have seven sacraments or two. You may in baptism be immersed or sprinkled. You may make regular confession of your sins to a priest who will set penances the doing of which will commute definite periods of your punishment in purgatory; or you may join a church which holds that there is no purgatory."

At about this point the convert, we may imagine, would revert to something like his pre-Christian impatience. "But which of them," he would cry, "is the true church? Which of them has taken its pattern from Christ?"

"Each of them claims that it does," the angel would answer.

Here, then, are five dimensions of Christianity—Christian ethics, the Christian gospel, Christian discipleship, Christian creeds, and Christian polities. Note now some differences between the first three of these dimensions and the last two. Most obviously, there is more general agreement among Christians with respect to the first three dimensions; the fourth and fifth cover the ground within which our major disagreements lie. The first three deal with the primary data of our faith, as found in the life and teaching of the Jesus of history who is the Christ of our experience; the last two are the products of reflection, interpretation, and organization. Again, the first three of these dimensions are accessible to every Christian as matters of direct experience, and are therefore verifiable by every follower of our Master. The creeds and polities are not so directly accessible and verifiable. One's convictions and practices in these dimensions are more largely dependent upon inference, tradition, authority, and social suggestion. Finally, the first three of these dimensions are vitally, organically related. In the abstract, they can be separated for purposes of thought and discussion; in actual practice, as principles of life, each tends to involve the other two. Taken together, they constitute the Christian gospel in the wider meaning of that term.

Two opposing tendencies are abroad in the churches today, both of which weaken their witness of the gospel of Christ.

One is the tendency to reduce Christianity to a single dimension, ethics merely; the other is to define it too rigidly in terms of the fourth and fifth dimensions.

Theoretically, the tendency to reduce Christianity to ethics is rooted in the pragmatic, naturalistic schemes of philosophy which have been so characteristic an expression of the life of our time; practically, it is associated with the movement toward a truer social interpretation and application of the principles of Jesus. The motives and purposes of the latter movement are good; but it cuts loose from its own dynamic when it tries, as a system of so-called humanism, to stand alone, without support in the eternal nature and purpose of God. Whatever else a Christian ethics without theistic faith may be, it is certainly not Christ's ethics, nor is the social gospel it promulgates Christ's gospel. For him, ethics and the gospel, man's duty and God's character, the way of life and the redeeming purpose and disposition of God, are indissolubly and organically related. A Christianity without the God who was in Christ, reconciling the world unto Himself, is no longer Christian.

The other tendency, which is not peculiar to our time, is to define Christianity in terms of a particular system of creeds or polities, and to exclude from Christian fellowship all who do not agree with these particular formulations or practices. So it often happens that sincere disciples of our Lord, endeavoring to walk in his way of love and service and experiencing the power of his gospel, may yet find that in the eyes of some they are not true Christians because they will not submit to the infallible authority of the Pope, or because they do not accept a particular theory of the atonement or of divine inspiration, or because they do not expect the visible, imminent, pre-millennial second coming of

Christ. Surely this is a misplacement of emphasis, to the
relative neglect of the weightier matters.

The population of Brazil is predominantly of the Roman
Catholic faith, but freedom is afforded to Protestant churches,
some of which are indigenous, while others are in part dependent upon missionary aid. The constituency of the
various Protestant churches totals some five hundred thousand; the Catholic, over thirty million. Yet I recently received a folder from one of the Protestant missionary societies—let us, for anonymity, call it the Fellowship Society.
It contained a map of Brazil with the places marked in
which churches of the Fellowship are located, and beneath
the map was this legend: "Population of Brazil, 40,000,000.
Membership of the Fellowship churches, 24,000. Souls to
be saved, 39,976,000."

In contrast let us recall the widely-quoted peroration of
one of the Chinese Christian leaders at the first meeting of
the National Christian Council of China, as he pleaded for
a Christian church in his country which would rise above
the differences of creed and polity that hold the churches
of America apart: "We are agreed to differ, but resolved to
love." I have been told that at the Indianapolis meeting of
the Northern Baptist Convention, when it was feared that
strife over theological issues might disrupt that body, this
sentence hung upon the wall of the convention hall. There
is something dramatic about that—more than dramatic, it is
soul-searching. Back from China comes the message to the
churches of America: "We are agreed to differ, but resolved
to love."

I do not mean to say that the fourth and fifth dimensions
are negligible. I am not pleading for the discarding of
doctrines and the blurring over of differences. The message

from China has two sides. It recognizes the agreement to differ as well as the resolve to love. I have scant sympathy with the popular decrying of theology. A religion without theology would be a religion without thought concerning the eternal verities. Shall we use the minds God gave us on all lesser subjects, but withhold them from thinking on the Highest? And, just because the Highest lies beyond their power fully to comprehend and describe, there is always room for honest differences of insight, conviction, and emphasis.

The world needs more, not less, thinking in the realm of the creeds as well as in the field of Christian social ethics. Intolerance is the fruit of ignorance. Clear thinking does not fear the fellowship of those who differ. The most jealous sectarianism is that of folk whose creeds and polities are matters of habit, custom, and contagion merely. The man who sees clearly the reasons for his own convictions is able to appreciate and respect the reasons which others have for their convictions. He is not afraid to cooperate with others, for he knows how far agreement goes and where difference begins, how important or how trivial the differences are, and what are the bearings of both agreements and differences upon those purposes of Christian love which we possess in common.

Yet when full acknowledgment has been made of the legitimacy and necessity of creeds and polities, the fact remains that the Gospel is primary. To forget that is to fall into legalism and institutionalism. We must keep right perspective. We must put first things first. The purpose of Christian missions is rightly conceived, not in terms primarily of the doctrines and forms of organization that lie within the fourth and fifth dimensions of Christianity, but in terms primarily of the first three of these dimensions. The purpose of missions is to share with others the gospel of Christ. Let them "express the gospel through their own genius and through forms suitable to their racial heritage." They will be no less our brethren.

IX.

THE MOTIVES OF MISSIONS

IN A MOVEMENT such as the Christian movement the matter of most vital importance is the motives that inspire it. What makes men give time, money, energy and life to the cause of Christian missions? Are the motives worthy? Are they valid? Will they bear scrutiny? Is the Christian mission movement of sufficient soundness at its heart that men may give themselves to it wholeheartedly?

This is no mere matter that concerns Christian missions alone. For if we find that we cannot share what we have in Christ with every man, then we will soon not be able to hold it at home. For what is not universal is not true. There is no such thing as local truth, for truth by its very nature is universal. The moment we discover truth we discover something that rises above national boundaries and belongs to everyone everywhere. There is no such thing as American science or Chinese mathematics. There is just science or just mathematics. When a truth is discovered in science it belongs to a race as such. It is not different in religion. If we discover truth in religion it belongs to man as man.

So if we find that we cannot share our faith with another it must be because of one of two reasons: either the faith is not true, hence not universal, or else it is not propagated with worthy motives. It is not the function of this chapter to deal with the question of the universality of the Christian faith, but only with the motives that inspire its propagation.

The movement is charged with being a species of imperialism. This charge of imperialism usually takes one of three forms. Some of the critics of Christianity say that it is the religious side of the Imperialisms of the West. They claim that Christian missions become the tools of pushing imperialism—that missions go ahead and open up the situation by schools, hospitals and kindliness in general, and then political imperialism comes along and takes over the situation in the name of empire.

While we cannot admit the full truth of this criticism, nevertheless we must admit that there is some truth in it. This was so at least in the beginnings of Christian missions during the modern era. In many cases there has been an alliance in thought and spirit. Much of it unconscious, of course. The underlying thinking in many minds was that Western civilization was Christian civilization and its extension was a part of the process of Christianizing the world. When Francis Xavier gave baptismal certificates to his converts in India, these certificates practically became passports of the Portuguese government and brought the convert under the protection of that government. Obviously no self-respecting nation could allow such a process to continue without protest. It is only fair to say that this process is over and belongs to a dead past. No longer could this or should this ever happen again.

Unjust and unequal treaties have been forced upon China because of the death or mistreatment of a foreign missionary. This meant, of course, that foreign powers were waiting for opportunities of this kind and used them to the full.

This brought forth the cry of the anti-Christian movement which swept through China a few years ago that the Christians are "the running dogs of the imperialists." While of course this was a gross exaggeration, nevertheless it had some truth in it. It has been said that when the white man went to Africa he had the Bible and the African had the land, but soon the African had the Bible and the white man had the land. This too is an exaggeration, but there is just enough truth in it to make it sting.

Ofttimes the missionary has stood with the ruling powers and become the voice of privilege rather than the voice of the people. Very often he sided in thought with Western powers because they were supposed to stand for Christianization.

While there is some truth in these charges, nevertheless we can now say that this period of alliance with imperialism, whether conscious or unconscious, is at an end. Unequal treaties will never again be forced upon China because of her treatment of missionaries. The whole tendency is now toward the undoing of anything of this kind. The Jerusalem Conference marked a stage in the dissolution of any bond which still bound Christian missions to imperialism. At that Conference it was decided to ask Western nations to withdraw military protection from missionaries and mission property.

It was a high moment when we asked that the message of the missionary should not be complicated with the sound of gunboats, that we desired to go at our own risk, that if we perished we perished, but that the truth we held and proclaimed would not perish, but would live on with greater power. We were rediscovering our original weapons—we would overcome evil with good, hate by love and the world by a cross of suffering. We would believe that our strongest backing would come, not from self-asserting Cæsar, but from the self-giving Christ. Two minutes after this resolution was passed Easter morning dawned—in more ways than one! The Christian movement will have a resurrection if it maintains its soul entirely free from Western imperialistic expansion and remains true to its own genius and uses its own weapons in conquering the world. We must show Christ standing, not as the representative of white rule, but as the brother of men.

If, therefore, the missionaries were sent out with any touch of political imperialism in the motive that sent us out, it is turning out badly for that motive, for we come back with a passion for the freedom of all men everywhere. We grant that imperialisms have often done an immense amount of good in spreading education, in bringing settled government to chaotic situations, in providing honest and upright officials and in preparing people for self-government. But there is no nation good enough to hold permanently another nation against its will. Freedom for all men is inherent in the Gospel and this freedom extends to all realms and includes the political. By the very nature of our Gospel we must stand with the weaker peoples in their demand for national self-expression. This does not mean that we should go as political partisans—the fact that we are guests of many national situations precludes that, but it does mean that we go inwardly disposed in sympathy toward the total rise of a people including the political.

Moreover, we should go with the outlook and spirit of preserving all that is fine and noble in the national culture of the nations to which we go. We should come actively encouraging the retention and preservation of anything worth while in the culture and religion of the people where we labor.

This does not mean that the end is to be a syncretism—an amalgam of all faiths. "Eclecticisms pick and choose, syncretisms combine, but only life assimilates." The Gospel repudiates an eclecticism, it refuses a syncretism, but it is life and it therefore assimilates. Just as a plant reaches down into the soil and gathers out elements that are akin to its own nature, and lifts them up into its own life and makes them into an entirely new organism, so the Gospel reaches down into the soul and soil of a people to which it goes and takes out elements akin to its nature and lifts them up into its life stream and transforms them into something new. The end is not a mere patchwork of truths put together, but an entirely new thing. The plant fashions these assimilated elements according to the laws of its own life, so the law of the spirit of life in Christ Jesus fashions assimilated elements according to its own genius and life.

Syncretism in philosophy belongs to the period of decay when philosophy can no longer create—it can only combine that which has been created. This is also true in religion. We therefore refuse syncretism because we believe that Jesus Christ is not decaying—He is still creative.

Syncretism would spell weakness and not strength. We must not tone down or accommodate Christ in the interest of a seeming broadness. We do not become more universal by becoming less Christian. The fact is that the more definitely Christian we are the more universal we are. The really Christian mind and attitude is universal, for we believe that they rest upon ultimate facts of our universe.

But would this attitude not stop progress in religion? We believe not. In every realm of life we discover an ultimate which becomes the beginning place of progress. The discovery that in mathematics that two and two made four did not stop mathematical progress; it began it. For upon this fixed ultimate vast mathematical calculations are being built up. The finding of an ultimate was the beginning of progress. Until we got something fixed—until we were sure that two and two made four and not five, we could not go on. In Jesus Christ we believe that we have discovered a moral and spiritual ultimate. Beyond Him we do not believe that this race will progress. But this does not stop progress. It begins it. For we find Christ is God's final, but unfolding Word.

Fresh light is breaking out from Him all the time. He fulfils all that is beautiful and true in the past of all peoples, but He also freshly creates, constantly and continuously. We are convinced then that the end of religion is not a patchwork, but a Personality—an infinitely unfolding Personality.

In Christ we are therefore saved from a cultural and national imperialism, because He preserves all that is fine in all nations, but we are also saved in Him from ending in the paralysis of a syncretism. He gives dynamic and driving force to our motive.

This has not always been our spirit. Again and again we have thought that we had to impose our Western culture along with our Gospel. But the process of separating the two has been going on apace. In the beginning we did not want to see good in these ancient cultures and religions, for we thought that if we did it would mean that these discovered goods would be reasons why we should not be there as missionaries. When I first went to India I did not want to find good in India's religions and culture. But the turning point came because of two things: first of all I had to acknowledge that there were beautiful and good and true things in the non-Christian faiths and cultures; and secondly, I saw that Jesus came not to destroy any of this, but to fulfil it. We could then look with sympathy and understanding upon any truth found anywhere. We were no longer mere iconoclasts, but preservers. It is true that a great deal would have to be destroyed, but nothing good or true.

The attitude of Christian missions and of Christian missionaries turned with sympathy to build any fine trait or truth into the new Kingdom of God which they were establishing. Perhaps it would be truer to say that these truths were already a part of the Kingdom which they proclaimed, imperfect and incomplete, but nevertheless a part of God's Kingdom. We began to realize that God was in these lands before we arrived and that He was at work before we began.

Christian missions now found themselves friends of national freedom and helpers and completers of national genius and truth. The charge of political and national imperialism is now largely irrelevant.

But, says the critic, if it isn't political imperialism isn't it denominational imperialism? Aren't Western denominations trying to build up vast denominations in order to gain prestige and power—a species of denominational megalomania?

There is some truth in this, for modern Christian missions grew up at the time of denominational expansion in the West. They therefore partook of denominational emphases. This has come out again and again. But if we were sent out through motives of denominational aggrandizement it is turning out very badly for that motive. For amid the struggle of things in the East we have seen issues so big that the lesser issues begin to fade out in the light of the larger ones. What real relevancy has the question of whether I am a Baptist or a Presbyterian or a Methodist or Episcopalean in the light of the question of whether Christ or some other shall hold the destiny of this race? When one sees the issue between Christ and materialistic communism, then the lesser issues sink into relative unimportance. The great issue is whether we are Christians in any really vital way, and not the question of whether we are Baptists or Methodists or some other.

Besides, we have discovered in our Round Table Conferences in the East that the Christian church is the most united body on earth. As we have asked the members of the Round Table Conferences to tell what religion is meaning in experience, we have discovered that when the Christians drop down beneath the level of organization and special doctrine to the level of experience, there the Christian church is really united. Wherever Christians are really Christians they are united in the deepest thing in life, namely in life itself. They actually share the same life. They do not have to strive for unity, they have it in the most fundamental facts. We have then the strange anomaly that the people who are most united at the depths are the most divided at the surface.

Again if you were to ask where we think the saints most thickly congregated, for the life of us, we could not say. They seem to be about equally distributed among all the denominations. There is no denomination that has any corner on the saints. God seems to work through the denomination—sometimes in spite of it, but never exclusively or particularly in any one of them. If this statements hurts our denominational pride it may help our Christian humility!

The pressure for unity is today coming from the mission

fields. So if we were sent out through the denominational motive it is turning out rather badly for that motive. For we find ourselves throwing the emphasis upon the fact of our being Christians rather than upon the fact of our belonging to some particular denomination. There are more unified projects in the mission field than at the home base. Christian missions, like flowing water, are dropping some of their extroneous matters gathered at the home base as they flow toward world needs.

This means that Christian missions are bringing pressure to bear upon the situation at home and abroad to do away with all overlapping, all competitions, all useless duplications within the Christian movement. For a divided church can have little moral authority in a divided world.

But a further criticism is made. If it isn't political or denominational imperialism, isn't it a species of spiritual imperialism? Isn't it a fussy desire to manage other peoples' souls in their supposed interests? That a good deal of this spirit is found in Christian work at home and abroad is not to be denied. It often satisfies one's sense of importance to play the brother bountiful to supposedly weaker peoples. Therefore Christian work is often the religious side of a superiority complex.

A great deal of our "training for leadership" smacks of this. Jesus said, according to Moffat, "Be ye not called leaders." The attitude of the leader is: "I lead and you follow"—an attitude which cannot be Christianized, for it is self-assertive. "He that saveth his life shall lose it." Trying to be a leader is a kind of self-saving and therefore of self-losing. We do not produce leaders out of this mentality. "Be ye called servants," said Jesus. This attitude can be Christianized. It is the losing of one's self in a human need and finding one's self in the process. So far as Christian missions have partaken of the leadership mentality, they have been on a false trail, but when they have produced servants, men and women who have lost themselves in meeting the needs of others they have to that extent been Christian. Missions must produce servants, not leaders. But in doing so these very servants will become leaders by the sheer force of what they are. Christian missions must go as the servants of the people for Jesus' sake. Then the servant of all will become the greatest of all.

There is another factor working against the spiritual imperialism mentality. We find that we succeed only as we make ourselves dispensable. We are there not merely to do a work, but to produce others who can do it. Our success then lies in the production of others who can take our places. Inherent in the process is something then that works against a possessive mentality. It is quite true that many missionaries have not yielded to this pressure and have maintained the possessive mentality concerning their work. This has resulted in the sterility of both themselves and their work. We must do as one national suggests, "Open the door and get out of the doorway."

"Now thank God, I've succeeded," said a very prominent Christian worker when he was told that an Indian had been appointed in his very responsible position.

We feel, therefore, if we are true to the genius of our Gospel and the inherent demand of our work we shall not be fussy managers of other people, but their servants for Jesus' sake. And Christian missions are increasingly partaking of this mentality. Sometimes we are forced to it by the pressure of circumstances and sometimes impelled by our own inward motives, but constantly driven by the Spirit of God to become like Him who came not to be ministered unto but to minister. Practically all the positions of authority in missions are in the hands of Japanese Christians; increasingly is authority being put upon the Chinese Christians where all the schools have Chinese at the head of them, and the same thing is happening in India but at a slower pace. When India gets her own self-government the pace will be accelerated by leaps and bounds.

There are several other criticisms of our motives which are not concerned specifically with the imperialistic mentality, but have to be met before our motives emerge clear and compelling. Mahatma Gandhi voices one such criticism when he says that there should be no conversions in religion. The feeling back of this objection is that we are still trying to gain prestige and power by numbers and that the whole thing smacks of a religious dominance. Mahatma Gandhi expressed this when he said to some American newspaper correspondents that "if the missionaries should use their schools and hospitals for the purposes of proselytism we should ask them to withdraw when we get our own self-government." This statement created a stir and Mahatma Gandhi explained his position, and in explaining it modified it, for his last word was, "Even under self-government the missionaries would be allowed to proselytize, but under the protest of such men as myself who feel that it is done in the wrong way."

We thank him for this clarification, but say in reply that we do not wish to proselytize. We feel there is something inherently unChristian in the whole proselytism mentality. Jesus was opposed to it. He said to the religious leaders of that day, "Ye compass land and sea to gain a proselyte and

then you make him twofold more a child of hell than yourselves." To Him the scramble for numbers was irreligious.
He opposed proselytism. But He insisted on conversion—
"except a man be converted he cannot see the Kingdom
of God."

Is there a valid distinction between proselytism and conversion? We believe there is. Proselytism is the change
from one group or sect or opinion to another without any
necessary change in character. It involves a change in label,
but not necessarily in life. Conversion on the other hand
involves a very definite and decisive change in character. In
the New Testament sense conversion is the reconstruction of
the sum total of life, the change of its inner fibre of being,
animating it with different motives and turning it toward
another goal. Now the chief need of life in East and West
is conversion. When Mahatma Gandhi said, "India is in
no need of conversion," he must have used "conversion"
in the sense of proselytism, for the fundamental need of all
men everywhere is conversion. We repudiate proselytism
but we insist upon conversion both for ourselves and others.
This is not a geographical, but a human need. As long as
Jesus Christ can produce the fact of conversion He will be
indispensible to human life and to proclaim Him a human
necessity.

If the Church loses this power to convert—to make bad
men into good men, weak men into strong men, moral
failures into moral victors—if it loses this power then it loses
its right to be called Christian. If this miracle of the
changed life is no longer a central and fundamental fact in
its impact upon the world, it has lost its function. For real
religion is the *Ought-to-be* standing over against the *Is*, chal-

lenging it, changing it and producing the fact of conversion. And when it can no longer do that it has abdicated its function.

But this conversion is not merely individual, it is social as well. The Kingdom of God is the ultimate order for human living in all its phases. It demands conversion both of the soul and of the social system. For evil can be in the individual will, it can be in the collective will. Shall we pick up the wounded in war or strike at the war system? Shall we rescue individual drunkards or strike at the liquor traffic? Obviously the answer is that we must do both. One without the other is incomplete. They must be held in a working blend. The motive of Christian missions must encompass both. The end would mean not social service alone, but social reconstruction. The Kingdom of God on earth demands a thorough-going renovation of the sum total of life in all its aspects.

No thoughtful person challenges the right and necessity for real religion to convert in this sense, but the changing of the outer allegiances brings the controversies. We believe that no change in outer allegiance should ever take place that is not based upon an inward change. But if the inner life has been really changed by Christ we feel that the man has a right to make outer changes that would correspond to that fact. For if the outer without the inner is hypocracy then the inner without the outer is also hypocracy. The only true life is the one that is inwardly and outwardly the same. If the inner life has become Christian then the outer allegiances and associations should also become Christian.

"Why do you get people to baptize them?" said a thoughtful Hindu to me one day. I replied, "I do not get anyone to baptize them. They have to get me to baptize them."

For when a man asks me to baptize him I always suggest that he stay with us and if he shows signs that Christ is being formed in Him and that life is really being changed, then I feel that he has a right to make the outer allegiance conform to that fact. But let us have no change of label that does not involve a change of life.

Perhaps it would be well to discuss here the question of whether schools and hospitals should have a conscious evangelistic purpose. If it is meant that they should be used as baits for evangelistic work, then the answer must be a decisive, *No*. Nothing should be used to gain ulterior ends. The whole thing must be open and frank and unashamed, or not at all. We believe that real education and healing are of themselves parts of the program of the Kingdom of God. They have a right to exist in and of themselves apart from any other purpose or motive. But to say that there should be no conscious evangelistic motive in education and medical work is to compartmentalize life. The whole of one's life and endeavor should express the evangelistic passion. We should not force our religion on anyone coming to us for education or for healing, or make it the price of receiving that healing or that education; but to say that we shall not share the deepest convictions of our lives frankly and freely is to impose upon us a guilty silence and to produce an air of unreality. We should give education and healing freely and frankly with no strings tied to it, but along with it we should just as freely and just as frankly let it be known what are the sources of the inspiration and life behind all our doing. To keep silence there is to make for falsity. If we do not believe in what we have, we should change it, but if we do believe in it, we should share it. All life that is really Christian should have a conscious and unconscious evangelistic purpose, for "no virtue is safe that is not enthusiastic"; no life is Christian that is not Christianizing.

But again Mahatma Gandhi expresses an objection: "If you are to carry on evangelistic work let it be by the rose-perfume method of evangelism. The rose exudes its perfumes and people come to it, drawn by the sweetness of its scent; there is no propaganda, the life does the drawing. Live this life and people will come and ask the source of it." This is an objection that must be seriously listened to. For there is no doubt that Christianity as organized in Western expressions is built too much on words. Our services are largely preaching. Our houses of worship are auditoriums. Someone asked a Chinese what he thought of Christianity and he replied, "It is a very talkie religion." So when Gandhi says there should be a moratorium on words we should heed what he says.

But while this criticism must be listened to, it cannot be accepted in its entirety. Jesus used the rose-perfume method of evangelism—He went about doing good. Men were drawn to Him when they saw that He did all things well. He lived the life and men felt the power of that life. But He did not stop there. He interpreted what He was doing —interpreted it in words. And the deeds of His life and the words of His lips were blended like the words and music of a song. They were one. What He was, what He did and what He said were put together and became the Word. To leave out any one of these elements would have been disastrous, to put them together was a Gospel.

In this we must listen to Mahatma Gandhi's criticism, but we must heed our own Master and follow Him.

But again Gandhi voices a criticism which goes deeper. He says that it is indelicate to speak of these things.

It lacks humility. Religion must be of the essence of humility.

From Gandhi's standpoint he is right. For he looks on religion as an attainment through a tremendous self-discipline. Of course if it is an attainment we cannot speak of it without indelicacy and a lack of humility. But to us as Christians religion is not primarily an attainment but an obtainment. It is an offer to us of the redemptive grace of God through Jesus Christ. It is a gift—unmerited and unearned. "By grace are you saved through faith and that not of yourselves; it is the gift of God." I do not mean to say that there is no discipline in the Gospel. There is a very deep discipline by the love of Christ. That love disciplines the inmost thought, the inmost aspiration so that it is a far deeper discipline than a self-discipline. I rationalize and excuse myself but this discipline by the love of Christ is imperious and without appeal.

So while it is true that the Gospel has its disciplines, nevertheless it is primarily an offer of redemption to men who have nothing to offer save their own bankruptcy. Since it is a gift we can, by the very nature of things, speak of it. Were it our own attainment we could not speak of it without a lack of humility, but since it is the gift of another we cannot refuse to speak of it without ingratitude. When we speak of it we are laying the tribute of our gratitude at the feet of Another. Freely we have received, freely we must give. We must therefore agree to differ cordially with Mahatma Gandhi in this matter, for by the very nature of our Gospel we must share it. Our marching orders are not built upon a special text, but upon the very texture of the Gospel we hold. We see no stopping place this side of the last man.

197

Just in here it might be well to say parenthetically that the statement of the Laymen's Report as to the motives of Christian Missions lacks a depth which I find in the Gospel when the Report says: "To seek with people of other lands a true knowledge and love of God, expressing in word and life what we have learned through Jesus Christ and endeavoring to give effect to His spirit in the life of the world."

Note the word "learned"—Christ is primarily the teacher. But when I came to Christ I did not come primarily to *learn* something, but to *receive* something. I stood as a penitent and wanted to receive release and forgiveness from what I was and what I had done. He was to me primarily a Saviour. I learn of Him, but I also live by Him—initially and continuously.

The Laymen in their Report ask us to let down tensions, to do away with areas of conflict with the non-Christian cultures and religions. We agree—up to a certain point. We must let down tensions between our civilization and the civilizations of the East. There was a time when we made Western civilization practically a part of our message. That time has gone by. We know now that Western civilization is only partially Christianized. There is no such thing as a Christian nation. There are Christianized individuals and groups, but as nations we have not yet built our collective life upon the mind and spirit of Jesus. So we say to the East, "Take as much from our civilization as you can work into your own purposes. It is at your disposal, but it is not our message." We let down the tension there.

Again we would say to the East, "We do not present to you a fixed system of Christianity as built up and embodied in our Western denominations. They represent more or less approximations to the mind of Christ. Take what you can from them. They are at your disposal. But you have a right to come to this Gospel in a first hand way and a right to express it corporately in forms that fit and suit your own genius and life. We do not set up a tension between our system and your system." There is much of truth and reality in our religious systems of the West. This will live on. It can be transplanted. The East will probably take more of it if we do not insist upon her taking it.

But there is one place where we do not hesitate to set up a tension and that point is between Jesus Christ and human need. We set it up first of all between Christ and our own souls. We find that tension is to us redemptive. Next we set up that tension between Christ and our civilization. We are in the same deep need of the saving power of Christ as others. Then what we would take for ourselves we would share with others.

We would share Him because He is the best we have. Had we anything better we would share that. But we have nothing better. We share with the East our automobiles, our radios and our tobacco. Shall we not share with them the best thing we have in our civilization? Or shall we proclaim to the world that we are mere materialists and have nothing to share save our material things?

But what right have you to force your opinions on others? None, if they are our opinions. But in Jesus Christ we feel that He is not our opinion of life, but God's revelation of His redemptive purpose for a race. We give this not as originators or owners of it, but as those who pass on what has been passed on to us.

"But," said a foreign student studying in one of our universities, "you never export a thing unless you have a surplus of that thing. Have you a surplus of Christianity in the

West that you dare export it?" This question was based upon a misunderstanding. Of course we have no surplus of Christianity in the West. But the attempt to share our Gospel is in reality a prayer for more of it for ourselves. For if an individual would concentrate on himself to make himself Christian and not share his life with others he would be de-Christianized in the process. He has to have a cause outside himself to complete himself. The same thing with a group and with a nation. The Christian missionary enterprise is the stretching out of hands of help to other peoples, but that stretching out of hands is a conscious or unconscious prayer that we might have more of it for ourselves.

"But," someone objects, "until it is fully operative at home, have we any right to give it to others?" Yes, because while we have no surplus to export there is a redemptive surplus in Christ that could redeem life in East and West. We proclaim Him—not ourselves.

We do not hesitate to export our science, though who would dare say we have fully organized our findings in science into our collective life? No one who is conscious of the haphazardness of that collective life. The body of scientific knowledge is far ahead of its organizational expression. But we follow on to bridge that gap. So in religion Christ is ahead of us. We know it. But this missionary movement to help others to the fullest life is part of the attempt to fill that gap. But that gap will always be there. For fresh light is breaking out from Him all the time. He is fixed in history but unfolding before us. It is becoming more and more demanding to be a Christian. He said to His disciples, "I have many things to say unto you but ye cannot bear them now, but when He the Spirit of Truth is come He will guide you into all truth for He shall take of the things of mine and shall show them unto you." Here He provided for a progressive revelation of Himself. He is God's final, but unfolding word.

But the deepest place in our motive is the cross. Someone has defined life as sensitiveness. In the lowest life, the mineral kingdom, sensitiveness is asleep, hence life is low. In the plant it awakens—plants respond to love and feel pain and gasp in death, according to Prof. Bose, whose delicate instruments have caught the responses of the plant. In the animal we have a wider range of sensitiveness, hence a higher type of life. In man we find a being who is often sensitive beyond the immediate circle of his own kinship, and in the highest ranges of man we find those who feel deeply for all men everywhere. In Jesus Christ we find the supreme sensitiveness, hence the supreme life. Every man's pain was His pain, every man's trouble His trouble and every man's sin His sin. He gathered it all up into His own heart upon the cross and there that heart broke because of an infinite sensitiveness. He died for us.

Here then is the central place of our motive, for the cross is God's love coming into contact with our sin and pain and crimsoning into suffering. We are Christian to the degree that we share that sensitiveness which the cross supremely shows. The Christian mission movement is one of the phases of the manifestation of that sensitiveness to human need. We cannot remain Christian unless we accept what that cross gives us and share with others the same spirit. Judged by this test the life of many in the churches is about the spiritual level of the vegetable. They have little sensitiveness to human need.

But if the cross is the center of our mission motive the resurrection is the light and power that lights up the motive and gives it vitality and victory. We feel that we are dealing with and proclaiming God's victorious Word. The worst has been met and conquered, hence we do not know how again to be discouraged or to be silent. In view of these mighty facts we cannot hold our peace, for if we did the stones would cry out.

Our message then is Jesus Christ. He to us is not a "symbol," but a fact—a redemptive fact. We ask men to try Him as a way of life in the same way we try any other hypothesis. If it does not work do not take Him. But we are convinced from experience that it does work—that Jesus Christ is saving to the degree that we respond to Him. We have found that His infallibility lies in this: if any man takes the way that Jesus asks him to take he will infallibly find God, infallibly find a new victorious and satisfying way to live.

We do not believe that this constitutes "meddling," or that it is a manifestation of "the imperialistic mind," for we are humbled at the very moment of our highest exultation that we have found the way to live—humbled that we are not more like the One to whom we give our hearts.

But we call Him a Saviour because He literally saves—saves us from ourselves, our sins, our despairs and then gives vision and dynamic for the remaking of the world according to the pattern of the Kingdom of God. Until we see something better we shall cleave to Him and shall share Him with all men everywhere. Up to this time we have seen nothing better. There seems to be nothing else on the horizon.

A personal experience may clarify our motives as missionaries. When I arose from my knees after three days of earnest seeking for the way of life and redemption I knew

I

I had found, the certainty was written across every fibre of my being. But the strangest thing of all was that my first impulse was to put my arms around the world and share this with everybody. I felt that everyone had a right to it and should know this. Five minutes before I had no such impulse, for I had nothing to share. But five minutes later a passion to share had taken possession of me.

That impulse is the germ of missionary passion. I cannot explain it, much less analyze it. I only know when I get in close fellowship with Him there comes an almost irresistible impulse to pass on what one sees and finds there. After these years I find my motive much the same as when I arose from my knees that memorable night. I still want to put my arms around the world and share with everyone what I find in Him. For in Him I see the hope of this race. In Him I see a Kingdom that would replace the present kingdoms founded on greed, exploitation and selfishness, in Him I see health for our bodies, light for our minds, love for our starved hearts, courage and victory for our defeated wills and redemption from our sins.

The motive and aim, then, of Christian missions is the production of Christ-like character in individuals and in society—this to be brought about (a) by moral and spiritual conversion obtained by faith in and fellowship with God through Jesus Christ His Son, our Lord and Saviour; (b) by the sharing of a brotherhood life, transcending and finally doing away with all distinctions of class and race in the new divine society, the Kingdom of God on earth; (c) by becoming witnesses, by the power of the Holy Spirit, of this new life to others.